Auditing Red Flags

Steven M. Bragg

AccountingTools®

Published by AccountingTools, Inc., Centennial, Colorado.

ISBN-13: 978-1-64221-357-7

For more information about AccountingTools® products, visit our Web site at www.accountingtools.com.

Table of Contents

Auditing Red Flags **1**

Introduction *1*

The Audit Risk Framework *3*

Fraud Fundamentals for the Auditor *6*

Red Flags in the Control Environment *10*

Red Flags in Entity-Level Risk Assessment *13*

Revenue Recognition Red Flags *17*

Cash and Treasury Red Flags *21*

Receivables Red Flags *25*

Inventory Red Flags *28*

Fixed Asset Red Flags *33*

Liability and Expense Red Flags *37*

General Ledger Red Flags *41*

Estimate and Valuation Red Flags *45*

Related Party Red Flags *49*

Going Concern Red Flags *54*

Information Technology Red Flags *59*

Analytical Procedure Red Flags *63*

Audit Evidence Red Flags *68*

Inquiry Red Flags *72*

Industry-Specific Red Flags *76*

Auditor Responses to Red Flags *84*

Documentation of Red Flags *88*

Communication of Red Flags *91*

Professional Judgement *95*

Case Studies in Auditing Red Flags *98*

Revenue Fraud Case Study 98

Inventory Manipulation Case Study 99

Cash Theft and Concealment Case Study 100

Related-Party Concealment Case Study 100

Management Override Case Study 101

Going Concern Warning Signs Case Study 101

Building an Audit Approach to Spot Red Flags *102*

Summary *106*

Glossary 108

Index 110

About the Author

Steven Bragg, CPA, has been the chief financial officer or controller of four companies, as well as a consulting manager at Ernst & Young. He received a master's degree in finance from Bentley College, an MBA from Babson College, and a Bachelor's degree in Economics from the University of Maine. He has been a two-time president of the Colorado Mountain Club, and is an avid alpine skier, mountain biker, and certified master diver. Mr. Bragg resides in Centennial, Colorado. He has written more than 300 books and courses, including *New Controller Guidebook*, *GAAP Guidebook*, and *Payroll Management*. He has also written *The Auditors* science fiction trilogy.

Steven maintains the accountingtools.com web site, which contains continuing professional education courses, the Accounting Best Practices podcast, and thousands of articles on accounting subjects.

Auditing Red Flags

Introduction

Auditing red flags are conditions, events, relationships, or behaviors that suggest the possibility of heightened risk in a financial statement audit. A red flag does not prove that fraud, error, or a control failure has occurred. Instead, it serves as a warning sign that the auditor should look more closely at a matter and consider whether additional procedures are needed. Red flags can arise from many sources, including unusual transaction patterns, weak internal controls, inconsistent explanations from management, unexpected analytical relationships, or external pressures on the entity. In practice, auditors encounter red flags at both the overall entity level and the individual account or transaction level. Their importance lies in their ability to direct attention to areas where the risk of material misstatement may be greater than initially assumed.

Red flags matter because an audit is fundamentally a risk-based process. Auditors do not examine every transaction, and they do not verify every possible source of misstatement. Instead, they allocate their time and effort toward areas that appear most likely to contain errors or intentional manipulation. Red flags help shape that allocation of effort. When warning signs emerge during planning, the audit team may revise its understanding of the entity, change its assessment of risks, increase staffing levels, or design more targeted procedures. When red flags arise during fieldwork, they may prompt expanded testing, deeper inquiry, or a reassessment of management's representations. In this way, red flags are not peripheral observations. They are central to the auditor's ability to perform an effective audit by focusing resources on the matters that warrant the greatest scrutiny.

It is important to distinguish between red flags and definitive evidence of a misstatement. A red flag is an indicator, not a conclusion. For example, a sharp increase in year-end sales may suggest premature revenue recognition, but it may also be explained by legitimate seasonal demand or the timing of a major contract. Similarly, delayed bank reconciliations may point to weak controls or possible concealment, but they may also result from staffing shortages or poor organization. The auditor must therefore avoid treating every red flag as proof of wrongdoing. At the same time, the auditor must avoid dismissing warning signs too quickly. The proper response is to investigate, corroborate, and evaluate. Audit quality depends on the ability to recognize when an issue is merely unusual and when it may indicate a material problem. That distinction can only be made through the careful analysis of evidence.

The auditor's responsibility is not to assume dishonesty whenever a warning sign appears, but it is also not to ignore suspicious circumstances. Auditing standards require the auditor to identify and assess risks of material misstatement, whether caused by error or fraud, and to design responses that address those risks. This responsibility includes paying attention to conditions that may indicate management bias, control deficiencies, improper accounting, or intentional manipulation. The auditor must gather sufficient appropriate evidence to determine whether the financial statements are fairly presented, and that process necessarily includes follow-up on red flags. If a warning sign suggests that management may be overriding controls, withholding information, or presenting transactions in a misleading manner, the auditor is expected to respond with greater skepticism and stronger procedures. The responsibility is therefore twofold: to notice the warning sign and to take it seriously enough to determine whether it has audit significance.

Professional skepticism is the mindset that makes red flag identification meaningful. Without skepticism, auditors may see unusual conditions and accept explanations too readily. With skepticism, auditors remain alert to evidence that contradicts management's assertions and to information that suggests documents, estimates, or narratives may not be reliable. Professional skepticism does not mean assuming that management is dishonest. Rather, it means maintaining a questioning mind and critically evaluating audit evidence. This is especially important when red flags appear in areas involving judgment, estimation, related-party relationships, or complex transactions. In such settings, the risk is not always obvious, and management's explanation may sound plausible even when it is incomplete or biased. A skeptical auditor resists the urge to settle for surface-level answers and instead asks whether the available evidence truly supports the accounting treatment or disclosure.

Red flag awareness is closely tied to audit experience, training, and discipline. Experienced auditors often recognize patterns that suggest increased risk, such as repeated manual journal entries near period-end, unusual fluctuations in margins, missing documentation, or defensiveness during inquiries. However, red flag awareness should not be left to instinct alone. It should be embedded in the audit approach through planning discussions, fraud brainstorming, analytical procedures, walkthroughs, and ongoing team communication. Junior auditors should be trained to recognize the difference between routine exceptions and more serious warning signs. Senior auditors should create an environment in which concerns are raised promptly and evaluated objectively. A red flag that is ignored by one team member may become the source of a major audit failure if it is never communicated upward.

In many audits, the most significant problems are not hidden behind a single dramatic event. They emerge through a pattern of smaller warning signs that, when viewed together, indicate a broader risk. A weak control environment, aggressive performance targets, unusual estimates, and inconsistent documentation may individually appear manageable. Collectively, they may point to a serious risk of misstatement. For this reason, auditors must evaluate red flags not only in isolation but also in combination. In essence, auditing red flags sets the foundation for the entire audit process. It reminds the auditor that unusual conditions deserve attention, that warning signs must be investigated rather than assumed away, and that skepticism is essential to sound judgment. By recognizing and responding appropriately to red flags, auditors improve their ability to detect material misstatements and to perform audits that are both efficient and reliable.

The Audit Risk Framework

The audit risk framework provides the structure that auditors use to identify where misstatements may occur and to decide how much evidence is needed in response. Auditors do not approach financial statements as a uniform body of information in which every account carries the same level of uncertainty. Instead, they assess the nature of the entity, its environment, its transactions, and its internal controls to determine where the greatest risks lie. This framework is essential because an audit is a risk-based engagement. The auditor must decide where misstatements are most likely, where they would matter most, and how the audit approach should change when warning signs appear. Red flags fit directly into this framework because they often reveal conditions that increase the likelihood of error, fraud, or unreliable reporting.

EXAMPLE

A construction company enters into customized long-term contracts for commercial buildings. The accounting for these contracts requires management to estimate total project costs, measure progress toward completion, and recognize revenue over time. This area has high inherent risk because the estimates can change significantly as labor conditions, material prices, subcontractor performance, and design revisions affect project costs. A small error in estimating total costs can materially distort both revenue and profit.

The company has strong internal controls. Project managers must update cost forecasts monthly, the accounting department compares actual costs to budgets, supervisors review contract change orders, and senior management approves significant estimate revisions. Internal auditors also test selected contracts during the year. In this setting, the inherent risk remains high because of the underlying complexity, but control risk may be moderate or low if these controls operate effectively.

However, the auditor discovers that reconciliations are not completed on time, one executive can approve and record change orders without review, and cost estimate revisions are rarely challenged. The auditor also notices a pattern of aggressive year-end adjustments that increase reported profit. These red flags suggest that the controls may not prevent or detect misstatements promptly. As a result, the auditor would assess control risk as high and expand substantive testing in this area.

A central part of the framework is the distinction between inherent risk and control risk. Inherent risk refers to the susceptibility of an assertion to misstatement before considering the effect of related controls. Some areas naturally carry more risk because they involve estimation, complexity, judgment, or unusual transactions. For example, fair value measurements, revenue recognition in customized contracts, and related-party transactions often involve higher inherent risk than straightforward cash receipts. Control risk refers to the possibility that the entity's internal controls will fail to prevent or detect a misstatement on a timely basis. Even when a transaction area is complex, strong controls can reduce the likelihood that a misstatement will remain uncorrected. Conversely, even a relatively simple area can become risky if controls are poorly designed or inconsistently applied. When auditors observe red flags such as the lack of segregation of duties, incomplete reconciliations, or unusual management override activity, they may conclude that control risk is higher than previously expected.

Auditors must also distinguish between fraud risk and error risk. Error risk arises from unintentional mistakes, such as mathematical errors, incorrect interpretations of accounting requirements, oversight, or breakdowns in routine processes. Fraud risk involves intentional acts designed to deceive, such as fictitious revenue, concealed liabilities, altered documentation, or the deliberate override of controls. This distinction matters because the audit response to suspected fraud is often more rigorous and more skeptical than the response to an ordinary mistake. Fraud risk may require additional unpredictability in testing, deeper inquiry, more extensive journal entry analysis, and greater attention to management representations. Red flags often help auditors determine whether an issue may involve intentional manipulation rather than simple carelessness. For example, a one-time posting error may suggest an error risk, while repeated end-of-period manual entries that improve earnings may indicate fraud risk. The auditor must evaluate not only what went wrong, but also whether the surrounding circumstances suggest intent.

EXAMPLE

A retail company closes its books at the end of each month. During the annual audit, the auditor finds that one inventory purchase was recorded at $540,000 instead of $450,000 because a staff accountant transposed digits while entering the invoice. The mistake overstated inventory and accounts payable, but the supporting documentation was complete, the amount was corrected after review, and there was no sign that anyone benefited from the error. This situation points to error risk, because it arose from an unintentional processing mistake rather than a deliberate attempt to mislead.

In addition, the auditor identifies several manual journal entries recorded on the last day of the reporting period that increase revenue and reduce expenses. These entries were posted by the controller, lack adequate support, and were reversed shortly after year-end. When questioned, management gives vague explanations and cannot produce convincing evidence that the transactions were valid. The entries also appear designed to meet a lender covenant and bonus target. In this case, the issue suggests fraud risk rather than error risk. The timing, earnings effect, unsupported documentation, and management involvement all indicate the possible intent to manipulate results. Consequently, the auditor responds with heightened skepticism and expanded fraud-focused procedures.

These considerations lead to the broader concept of the risk of material misstatement. This is the risk that the financial statements are materially misstated before the auditor performs substantive procedures. It exists at both the financial statement level and the assertion level. At the financial statement level, risks may arise from weak governance, poor ethical culture, or significant economic pressure on management. At the assertion level, the focus narrows to specific balances, disclosures, and transaction classes. A material misstatement may relate to existence, completeness, valuation, rights and obligations, presentation, or cutoff. Red flags help the auditor connect general concerns to specific assertions. For example, slow-moving inventory may raise a valuation concern, while unusual credit memos issued after year-end may affect revenue cutoff and existence, and missing vendor invoices may signal completeness issues in accounts payable. By identifying these links, the auditor translates broad warning signs into targeted audit risks that can be addressed with evidence.

Red flags also influence the scope and nature of audit procedures. Scope refers to the extent of testing, including the size of samples, the number of locations visited, and the depth of follow-up performed. Nature refers to the type of procedures selected, such as inquiry, inspection, confirmation, recalculation, observation, or substantive analytical review. Timing also matters, since high-risk issues may require more work at year-end rather than at an interim date. When auditors encounter significant red flags, they usually respond by increasing the persuasiveness of the evidence obtained. They may expand testing, obtain more third-party evidence, perform surprise procedures, or assign more experienced personnel to the area. For example, if receivables appear overstated, the auditor may increase confirmation work and review subsequent cash receipts more extensively. If journal entry patterns appear unusual, the auditor may perform a more detailed data analysis of entries posted by certain users or during certain periods. Thus, red flags affect not only the auditor's risk assessment but the design of the audit itself.

EXAMPLE

A manufacturing company has operations in three locations. During preliminary procedures, the auditor notices several red flags involving accounts receivable. Days sales outstanding have increased sharply, a large number of sales were recorded in the final week of the year, and credit memos issued after year-end are unusually high. In addition, one branch office accounts for a disproportionate share of year-end sales growth. These indicators suggest a risk that receivables and revenue may be overstated.

Because of these red flags, the auditor changes the design of the audit. The scope of testing is expanded by increasing the sample of year-end sales transactions, selecting more customer balances for confirmation, and visiting the branch office that generated the unusual sales spike. The auditor also performs more detailed follow-up on subsequent cash receipts and examines supporting documents for sales recorded close to year-end. The nature of procedures changes as well. Instead of relying primarily on inquiry and analytical procedures, the auditor places greater emphasis on external confirmations, the inspection of shipping documents, and cutoff testing. Timing also shifts, with more work performed at year-end rather than earlier in the audit cycle. The engagement partner assigns a more experienced manager to review revenue testing. In this way, the red flags directly affect the scope, nature, and timing of audit procedures.

The final step is linking red flags to specific audit responses in a disciplined way. This connection is critical, because identifying a red flag has little value unless it leads to an appropriate action. The auditor should document the warning sign, identify the affected assertions, evaluate the possible causes, and determine what additional work is needed. A weak control over approvals may lead to more substantive testing of disbursements. A pattern of inconsistent explanations from management may lead to greater reliance on external corroboration. Aggressive estimates may require the involvement of a specialist or the development of an independent expectation. In this way, the audit risk framework turns observations into decisions. It prevents red flags from being treated as informal concerns and instead incorporates them into a structured process of risk identification, assessment, and response.

An effective auditor does not treat the audit risk framework as a mechanical checklist. It is a method of thinking that helps the auditor remain alert to where misstatements are most likely and how audit effort should be allocated. Red flags are especially important within this framework because they provide practical signals that risk may be changing. As new information emerges, the auditor may need to revise prior assumptions and alter the audit approach accordingly. That flexibility is essential to audit quality. A well-executed risk assessment does not eliminate uncertainty, but it helps ensure that the auditor responds intelligently and proportionately to the conditions encountered. In that sense, the audit risk framework is the foundation on which effective red flag analysis rests.

Fraud Fundamentals for the Auditor

An understanding of fraud fundamentals is essential to the effective identification and evaluation of auditing red flags. Auditors are not expected to guarantee that all fraud will be detected, but they are expected to assess the risk of material misstatement arising from fraud and to respond appropriately when warning signs appear. Fraud differs from ordinary error because it involves intentional deception. That intent may be directed toward misstating financial results, concealing the theft of assets, or obtaining improper business advantages through corrupt conduct. Because fraud can take many forms, auditors must understand its common patterns, the circumstances in which it tends to arise, and the ways in which it may be concealed. A solid grasp of fraud fundamentals allows the auditor to recognize when unusual conditions may reflect deliberate misconduct rather than simple carelessness or weak process execution.

Fraud affecting financial statements generally falls into several broad categories. One category is asset misappropriation, in which employees, managers, or others steal cash, inventory, supplies, or other resources belonging to the entity. Another category is fraudulent financial reporting, in which management or employees intentionally manipulate accounting records, estimates, classifications, or disclosures to present a false picture of financial performance or condition. A third category involves corruption, such as bribery, kickbacks, conflicts of interest, bid rigging, or other improper arrangements that may not always create immediate misstatements in obvious ways but which can expose the entity to losses, legal liability, and distorted accounting. In some situations, these categories overlap. For example, an employee who steals inventory may also alter inventory records to conceal the theft, thereby turning an asset misappropriation into a financial reporting issue as well. Auditors must therefore look beyond labels and consider how fraudulent conduct might affect specific assertions in the financial statements.

Asset misappropriation schemes are often the most common type of fraud within organizations, though they may not always produce the largest dollar losses on the financial statements. These schemes can involve the theft of incoming cash, fraudulent disbursements, payroll fraud, expense reimbursement abuse, check tampering, inventory theft, or the misuse of company assets. In many cases, the perpetrator attempts to hide the theft by falsifying supporting documents, altering reconciliations, or exploiting weaknesses in the segregation of duties. For example, an employee who controls both cash receipts and recordkeeping may divert funds and adjust customer balances to conceal the shortage. Similarly, a person with authority over vendor setup and payment processing may create fictitious vendors and approve payments to personal accounts. Asset misappropriation often thrives where oversight is limited, documentation is weak, and routine reconciliations are either not performed or not reviewed. Auditors should therefore regard weak custody controls, unusual adjustments, unexplained shortages, and inconsistent supporting records as potential indicators of this type of fraud.

Fraudulent financial reporting presents a different and often more significant threat to the audit because it can result in material misstatement of the financial statements as a whole. This type of fraud usually involves intentional efforts to overstate revenue, understate expenses, conceal liabilities, inflate asset values, or manipulate disclosures in order to meet earnings targets, satisfy debt covenants, influence stock prices, or preserve management compensation. Techniques may include recording fictitious sales, accelerating revenue recognition, deferring expenses, misclassifying transactions, using unsupported estimates, or omitting required disclosures. Unlike many asset misappropriation schemes, fraudulent financial reporting is often driven by senior personnel who have the authority to influence accounting decisions and override established controls. It may be carefully planned and supported by plausible explanations, which makes it especially difficult to detect. Auditors should be alert to patterns such as aggressive year-end entries, unexplained improvements in financial results, unusual relationships between financial and nonfinancial data, and resistance to audit inquiry in sensitive areas.

EXAMPLE

From 1999 to 2002, WorldCom used more than $9 billion of false or unsupported accounting entries to produce desired financial results, making it one of the largest accounting frauds in U.S. history. Much of the fraud involved improperly shifting ordinary "line cost" expenses into asset accounts, which reduced expenses and overstated profit. WorldCom announced in June 2002 that it would restate its financial statements after identifying billions of dollars of transfers that were not in accordance with GAAP.

This case illustrates why fraudulent financial reporting is especially dangerous to auditors. The misconduct was directed by senior executives, and the SEC alleged that Bernard Ebbers and others engaged in a scheme to conceal WorldCom's true operating and financial results, including manipulating revenue, expenses, and disclosures. The SEC also alleged that management gave false representations to the auditors and concealed the true accounting treatment being used.

For an auditor, WorldCom shows the importance of treating certain patterns as major red flags: aggressive efforts to "hit the numbers," unsupported year-end entries, management override, weak internal controls, and explanations that appear plausible on the surface but conceal intentional manipulation. The fraud ultimately led to bankruptcy and severe investor losses, showing how pervasive fraudulent reporting can affect the financial statements as a whole.

Corruption and bribery indicators are also important components of fraud awareness, even when their effect on the financial statements is indirect or concealed within ordinary accounts. Corruption includes schemes in which someone uses a position of authority for improper personal gain, often at the expense of the organization. Examples include employees accepting kickbacks from vendors, managers steering business to related parties, or procurement personnel manipulating bidding processes in exchange for favors or payments. Bribery may involve improper payments to customers, government officials, or intermediaries to secure contracts, approvals, or preferential treatment. These acts may be disguised as consulting fees, commissions, marketing costs, travel expenses, or other routine expenditures. Warning signs can include unusually close relationships with vendors, repeated use of the same intermediaries without clear justification, payments to offshore accounts, vague descriptions in disbursement records, or contracts awarded under irregular circumstances. Although corruption may not always produce an immediate material misstatement, it can distort expense recognition, conceal related-party issues, create contingent liabilities, and raise serious concerns about the integrity of management and the control environment.

EXAMPLE

Siemens AG resolved U.S. charges involving a widespread bribery scheme in 2008. The SEC and Department of Justice (DOJ) said Siemens used off-the-books slush funds, shell entities, and false entries to conceal improper payments made to obtain business in multiple countries. Authorities specifically alleged that bribes were often recorded as consulting fees, business services, or other seemingly routine expenditures, which is exactly why corruption can be difficult for auditors to spot when reviewing ordinary expense accounts.

From an audit perspective, Siemens is a strong corruption-warning example because the financial statement effect was often indirect rather than obvious. The issue was not simply one large account labeled "bribes." Instead, improper payments were hidden within normal disbursement categories and supported by fake consulting arrangements, offshore intermediaries, and misleading documentation. The DOJ also described weaknesses in internal controls and false entries in the company's books. For an auditor, the red flags would have included the repeated use of intermediaries without a clear business purpose, vague payment descriptions, unusual cross-border transfers, and management's willingness to circumvent approval processes. These indicators would raise concerns not only about possible illegal acts, but also about misstated expenses, undisclosed contingent liabilities, related-party concerns, and a weak control environment shaped by poor tone at the top.

To understand why fraud occurs, auditors often rely on the fraud triangle and the fraud diamond. The fraud triangle identifies three conditions commonly present when fraud occurs: pressure, opportunity, and rationalization. Pressure refers to a perceived need or incentive, such as financial stress, unrealistic performance expectations, personal debt, or fear of job loss. Opportunity arises when internal controls are weak, oversight is ineffective, or authority is concentrated in a way that allows misconduct to occur and remain undetected. Rationalization is the mental process by which the perpetrator justifies the act, perhaps by believing that the fraud is temporary, deserved, harmless, or necessary for the good of the business. The fraud diamond adds a fourth factor, capability, which recognizes that not everyone facing pressure, opportunity, and rationalization has the ability to carry out and conceal a fraud. Capability may involve technical skill, access, intelligence, confidence, and the ability to influence others or exploit systems. For auditors, these models are useful not because they predict fraud with certainty, but because they help identify environments in which the risk is elevated. When several of these elements are present, red flags should be evaluated with greater care.

Management override of controls is one of the most significant fraud risks that auditors face, because even well-designed control systems can be circumvented by those with sufficient authority. Management may override controls by approving improper journal entries, altering estimates, directing employees to bypass established procedures, suppressing documentation, or influencing the timing and classification of transactions. The risk is especially acute because override often occurs in areas requiring judgment, where explanations may appear reasonable on the surface. For example, management might instruct staff to record revenue before all performance obligations have been satisfied, delay the recognition of known liabilities, or adjust reserves using unsupported assumptions. Override can also occur through selective disclosure, such as withholding information about side agreements, contingent obligations, or related-party relationships from the auditors.

Auditing standards recognize that management override as a presumed risk in every audit, which means the auditor must respond to it regardless of whether specific suspicions already exist. This response commonly includes examining journal entries and other adjustments, reviewing accounting estimates for bias, and evaluating the business rationale for significant unusual transactions. However, the technical procedures alone are not enough. Auditors must also consider behavioral and environmental signals associated with override, such as dominant executives, a culture of fear, unusual secrecy, hostility toward questions, or pressure to achieve short-term financial targets. When these conditions exist, even routine accounting decisions may warrant closer scrutiny. Management override is dangerous precisely because it can make ordinary controls appear effective while critical exceptions are concealed from view.

Fraud fundamentals form a core part of audit judgment. They help auditors distinguish between routine irregularities and warning signs that may indicate intentional deception. By understanding the types of fraud that affect financial statements, the mechanisms through which they are carried out, the motives and conditions that support them, and the special risk posed by management override, auditors are better prepared to recognize red flags and design appropriate responses. This foundation is essential to a high-quality audit because fraud rarely announces itself openly. It is more often revealed through patterns, inconsistencies, pressures, and behaviors that only a knowledgeable and skeptical auditor will recognize as significant.

Red Flags in the Control Environment

The control environment is the foundation on which the rest of an organization's internal control system is built. It reflects management's attitude toward integrity, accountability, compliance, and financial reporting discipline. When the control environment is strong, employees are more likely to follow established procedures, raise concerns when problems arise, and treat internal controls as an essential part of operations rather than as an administrative burden. When the control environment is weak, formal policies may still exist, but they are less likely to function effectively in practice. For auditors, weaknesses in the control environment are especially important because they often signal elevated risk across multiple financial statement areas. A poor control environment does not prove that fraud or material misstatement exists, but it increases the likelihood that errors will occur, warning signs will be ignored, and intentional misconduct will go undetected.

One of the most significant red flags in the control environment is a weak tone at the top. Tone at the top refers to the example set by senior leadership regarding ethical conduct, transparency, compliance, and financial reporting reliability. Employees often take their cues from management's behavior rather than from written policies. If senior executives emphasize results at any cost, dismiss control procedures as obstacles, or tolerate questionable conduct by high performers, the message conveyed throughout the organization is that control discipline is secondary to short-term outcomes. This type of environment encourages rationalization, weakens accountability, and increases the risk that improper accounting or concealment of problems will occur. Auditors should pay close attention to signs that management does not consistently reinforce ethical expectations. Examples may include repeated exceptions to policy for favored individuals, dismissive attitudes toward compliance personnel, tolerance for aggressive accounting positions without strong support, or a lack of meaningful consequences for misconduct. A weak tone at the top often affects the entire organization, because it shapes the attitudes and decisions of everyone below senior management.

Another important warning sign is dominant management behavior. A strong leader is not necessarily a control problem, but management becomes a red flag when authority is overly concentrated, dissent is discouraged, and major decisions are driven by one or two individuals without meaningful challenge. In such situations, employees may hesitate to question unusual transactions, accounting judgments, or policy exceptions because they fear retaliation or believe that objections will be ignored. Dominant managers may pressure staff to achieve desired financial results, override normal approval processes, or restrict access to information. This behavior is especially concerning when the dominant individual is closely involved in accounting decisions, since that increases the risk of intentional misstatement or concealment. Auditors may observe this issue through tense interactions during meetings, highly scripted responses to inquiries, reluctance by employees to speak freely, or a pattern in which unusual transactions are always linked to executive direction. Dominant management behavior undermines the balance of authority that internal control systems require, and it can render otherwise well-designed controls ineffective.

A lack of segregation of duties is one of the most classic and persistent red flags in the control environment. Segregation of duties exists to prevent one individual from controlling an entire transaction cycle from initiation, to recording, to custody of the related asset. When those responsibilities are combined, the opportunity for error or fraud increases substantially because the same person can both commit and conceal an improper act. For example, an employee who can set up vendors, approve invoices, and process payments has the ability to create fictitious disbursements. A person who handles cash receipts and also records customer payments may divert funds and alter the accounting records to hide the theft. Smaller organizations often face practical limitations in staffing, but the absence of perfect segregation does not eliminate the need for compensating controls such as owner review, independent reconciliations, or detailed exception monitoring. Auditors should evaluate not only whether duties are formally segregated, but also whether the segregation works in practice. System access rights, shared passwords, inadequate review, and informal workarounds can defeat apparent separations of responsibility. Where segregation is weak, the auditor may need to increase substantive testing and place less reliance on internal controls.

Poor governance oversight is another major control environment red flag. Governance oversight refers primarily to the role of the board of directors, audit committee, or similar body in monitoring management, overseeing financial reporting, and ensuring accountability. Effective governance requires independence, competence, engagement, and a willingness to challenge management when necessary. When oversight is poor, management may operate with too little scrutiny, especially in areas involving estimates, related-party transactions, executive compensation, or unusual business arrangements. Warning signs may include infrequent board or audit committee meetings, limited financial expertise among those charged with governance, the superficial review of significant accounting matters, or excessive reliance on management's explanations without probing questions. In some organizations, governance bodies exist largely in form rather than substance. Minutes may be prepared, meetings may occur, and reports may be circulated, yet there may be little evidence of substantive oversight. Auditors should consider whether those charged with governance appear informed, independent, and actively engaged in matters affecting financial reporting. Weak governance increases the risk that problems identified by lower-level personnel, external auditors, or compliance staff will not receive appropriate attention.

An inadequate internal audit function can also signal a weak control environment. Internal audit serves as an important monitoring mechanism by evaluating controls, identifying process weaknesses, and reporting deficiencies to management and governance personnel. When this function is under-resourced, poorly structured, or lacking in independence, the organization loses a key layer of defense against error and misconduct. In some cases, internal audit may exist only nominally, with limited staffing, restricted access, or a narrow focus that excludes high-risk areas. In other cases, the function may report too directly to management whose work it is supposed to evaluate, reducing its objectivity. Auditors should consider whether internal audit performs meaningful reviews, whether recommendations are followed up, and whether significant findings are communicated promptly and acted upon. A weak internal audit function does not automatically create a misstatement, but it does reduce the organization's ability to identify and correct control failures internally before they affect the financial statements.

Ineffective whistleblower mechanisms are another important red flag because they affect whether employees feel safe reporting concerns. A whistleblower mechanism may include anonymous hotlines, reporting portals, direct access to the audit committee, or formal anti-retaliation policies. These systems are valuable because employees often observe misconduct, control bypasses, or suspicious behavior before external auditors do. However, the system is only effective if employees trust it. If complaints are ignored, confidentiality is weak, retaliation is tolerated, or reporting channels are not well communicated, employees may stay silent even when serious problems exist. Auditors should be alert to signs that reporting systems are not functioning as intended, such as a complete absence of complaints in a high-risk environment, vague explanations about complaint handling, or evidence that reported issues are not investigated thoroughly. An ineffective whistleblower mechanism deprives the organization of an early warning system and allows control problems to persist longer than they otherwise would.

EXAMPLE

According to U.S. enforcement filings, Siemens Argentina used purported consulting firms and intermediaries to channel corrupt payments connected to Argentina's national identity card project. The payments were not recorded as bribes. Instead, they were disguised as legitimate commissions and business consulting fees, supported by sham invoices and backdated authorization memoranda.

On the surface, the disbursements could have appeared to be ordinary vendor or consulting expenses. In reality, the filings alleged that some of the money was intended for government officials to help Siemens obtain, retain, or reinstate the contract. The SEC and DOJ also said Siemens had inadequate internal controls and improper practices that allowed these transactions to be concealed within normal accounting systems.

For an auditor, the warning signs would have included the repeated use of intermediaries without clear services, vague payment descriptions, unusual foreign accounts, and documentation that looked manufactured after the fact. Even if the immediate financial statement effect seemed limited to expense classification, the broader implications included illegal acts, false records, contingent liabilities, and serious concerns about management integrity and the control environment.

Taken together, these red flags reveal that the control environment is not merely an abstract concept. It has direct implications for audit risk and audit strategy. Weak tone at the top, dominant management, poor segregation of duties, weak governance, inadequate internal audit, and ineffective whistleblower systems all increase the likelihood that errors and fraud can occur and remain undetected. For auditors, these conditions warrant heightened skepticism, closer evaluation of control reliance, and a more carefully targeted audit response.

Red Flags in Entity-Level Risk Assessment

Entity-level risk assessment focuses on the broad conditions that can affect the reliability of an organization's financial reporting. While auditors must examine individual accounts and assertions, they also need to understand the larger business environment in which accounting decisions are made. Many of the most significant audit risks do not begin with a single transaction. They arise from pressures, incentives, structural complexity, and environmental conditions that influence management behavior across the organization. These entity-level conditions can increase the likelihood of error, encourage aggressive reporting, weaken internal control performance, or create opportunities for fraud. For that reason, auditors should pay close attention to red flags that appear at the overall business level, since they often shape the risk profile of the audit before detailed testing even begins.

One of the most common entity-level red flags is rapid growth or unusual profitability. Growth is not inherently suspicious, and strong profits may reflect sound strategy or favorable market conditions. However, when an entity grows faster than its industry, reports margins far above competitors, or achieves unexpectedly strong results during difficult economic periods, the auditor should consider whether those outcomes are fully supported by operational reality. Rapid growth can strain systems, overwhelm accounting personnel, and expose weaknesses in controls that were designed for a smaller organization. It may also create pressure to maintain the appearance of continued success, especially when investor expectations, lending arrangements, or compensation targets are tied to performance. In such circumstances, management may become more willing to adopt aggressive accounting positions or delay the recognition of adverse developments. Unusual profitability can also indicate that expenses are understated, reserves are inadequate, or revenue recognition practices are overly aggressive. The auditor should therefore compare reported performance with industry trends, operational capacity, cash flow patterns, and nonfinancial indicators to determine whether the results are plausible.

EXAMPLE

Luckin Coffee told investors that it had achieved rapid expansion after starting operations in October 2017, and by September 30, 2019 it reported 3,680 stores in 43 cities and 30.7 million cumulative transacting customers. It also reported third-quarter 2019 product revenue growth of 557.6% over the prior-year quarter. On its face, that kind of explosive growth could suggest a successful business model, but it also fit a classic entity-level red flag: performance rising so quickly that auditors should test whether the results were supported by cash flow, operations, and reliable underlying records.

The SEC later alleged that from at least April 2019 through January 2020, Luckin intentionally fabricated more than $300 million in retail sales by using related parties to create false transactions. The SEC also alleged that employees tried to conceal the fraud by inflating expenses, creating a fake operations database, and altering accounting and bank records.

For an auditor, Luckin shows why rapid growth and unusually strong reported results should be compared with operational capacity, independent evidence, and nonfinancial data. When reported expansion appears extraordinary, the auditor should consider whether the growth is genuine, whether controls kept pace, and whether pressure to sustain momentum encouraged aggressive or fraudulent reporting.

Financial pressure on management is another major red flag because it creates incentives that may distort financial reporting. Pressure can arise from many sources, including debt covenant requirements, declining liquidity, pending refinancing efforts, investor expectations, planned stock offerings, bonus arrangements, private equity exit strategies, or the need to avoid violating contractual obligations. Management facing intense financial stress may not begin with an intent to commit fraud, but it may rationalize aggressive assumptions, delay loss recognition, or present estimates in a more favorable light. The risk becomes greater when the entity has limited access to new capital, worsening operating results, or significant fixed obligations that cannot easily be reduced. Auditors should consider not only whether the business is under pressure, but also how visible and immediate that pressure is to senior decision makers. A company struggling to meet payroll, negotiate with lenders, or preserve its market valuation may face incentives that affect multiple accounting areas, including revenue recognition, impairment analysis, reserves, and going concern disclosures. Financial pressure does not prove misstatement, but it significantly elevates the risk that management judgment will be biased.

Complex organizational structures also deserve careful attention during entity-level risk assessment. Complexity can arise from multiple subsidiaries, foreign operations, special-purpose entities, holding companies, layered ownership arrangements, joint ventures, or decentralized reporting systems. In some businesses, complexity is a natural consequence of growth, regulation, or cross-border operations. Even so, it creates audit risk because it can obscure accountability, complicate consolidation, reduce transparency, and make it more difficult to determine whether transactions have economic substance. Complex structures may also increase the likelihood that significant intercompany activity, related-party transactions, contingent obligations, or off-balance-sheet arrangements are not fully understood or properly reported. The more layers an organization has, the more opportunities there are for inconsistent accounting, incomplete disclosures, and weak oversight. Auditors should be especially alert when management cannot clearly explain how entities relate to one another, when reporting lines are confusing, or when the organization uses entities that appear to have a limited operational purpose. Structural complexity does not automatically imply wrongdoing, but it often creates an environment in which important risks can be concealed more easily.

EXAMPLE

Enron relied heavily on special purpose entities (SPEs) and other complex structures to move assets and liabilities off its balance sheet and present its financial position more favorably. The SEC later alleged that Enron transferred assets and liabilities to SPEs so that the activities would be treated as "off-balance-sheet," while congressional materials noted that these structures could obscure leverage and economic exposure from investors and other users of the financial statements.

From an audit standpoint, Enron shows why structural complexity is an entity-level red flag. The organization used multiple entities, overlapping transactions, and confusing arrangements that made it harder to determine who bore the real risks and whether the transactions had economic substance. A Senate report noted concerns about Enron's highly structured transactions with multiple SPEs and the risk that the overall structure could fail if one element broke down. The SEC also alleged that by 1999 Enron had become increasingly dependent on SPE transactions to meet its financial reporting goals.

For an auditor, this is exactly the danger described in risk assessment guidance: when management cannot clearly explain how entities relate to one another, or when entities seem to exist mainly to achieve accounting results, complexity may be concealing significant related-party transactions, off-balance-sheet obligations, and incomplete disclosures.

Related-party influence is another entity-level red flag because it can affect both the substance of transactions and the objectivity of decision making. Related parties may include owners, executives, affiliates, family members, controlled entities, or other parties able to exert significant influence over the organization. Transactions involving related parties are not inherently improper, but they deserve careful scrutiny because they may not occur on arm's-length terms and may be used to shift profits, conceal obligations, manipulate results, or disguise the true nature of economic relationships. At the entity level, related-party influence becomes especially concerning when major decisions are concentrated among individuals with overlapping personal and business interests, or when significant transactions repeatedly involve parties connected to management. Warning signs include vague disclosures, undocumented arrangements, unusual pricing, or reluctance to discuss ownership relationships in detail. Auditors should evaluate whether related-party influence affects governance, approval processes, financing arrangements, or operational decisions, since these factors may have broad implications for financial reporting risk.

EXAMPLE

According to the SEC, members of the Rigas family, who founded and controlled Adelphia Communications, caused the company to engage in numerous undisclosed related-party transactions and to omit massive related obligations from its financial reporting. The SEC alleged that Adelphia excluded more than $2.3 billion in bank debt from its consolidated balance sheets even though Adelphia was jointly liable, and also failed to disclose extensive dealings between the company and entities controlled by the Rigas family.

This is exactly why related-party influence is an entity-level red flag. The issue was not simply that related parties existed. The problem was that ownership, management authority, and affiliated entities were so intertwined that business decisions and financing arrangements were no longer clearly separate or objective. When the same family effectively controlled the company and related entities, transactions could be structured in ways that obscured the true economic substance and concealed obligations from investors.

For an auditor, the red flags would have included concentrated decision-making power, vague or incomplete related-party disclosures, unusual financing arrangements, and reluctance to explain affiliated relationships clearly. Those conditions create heightened risk that governance, approvals, and financial reporting have been influenced by personal interests rather than arm's-length business judgment.

Frequent changes in strategy or leadership can also signal elevated entity-level risk. Strategic changes such as a sudden expansion into new markets, major restructuring, repeated acquisition activity, or shifts in business model may place strain on accounting systems and increase the likelihood of reporting errors. New leadership can bring legitimate improvements, but frequent turnover in key roles such as the chief executive officer, chief financial officer, controller, or head of internal audit may suggest instability, internal conflict, or dissatisfaction with financial reporting practices. Leadership changes can disrupt continuity, delay control activities, and alter reporting priorities in ways that increase audit risk. They may also indicate that knowledgeable personnel have left during periods of stress or disagreement. Auditors should consider the timing, frequency, and context of these changes. For example, the departure of accounting personnel during a challenging reporting period, or the repeated replacement of executives responsible for accounting oversight, may warrant heightened skepticism and closer inquiry into the reasons behind the turnover.

Industry instability and economic stress are broader environmental factors that often shape entity-level risk in important ways. A company may have strong internal processes, yet still face significant reporting pressure if it operates in a declining industry, an overcapacity market, or a sector exposed to volatile demand, commodity price swings, regulatory disruption, or technological obsolescence. Economic stress can reduce revenue visibility, compress margins, impair asset values, and increase uncertainty in estimates. It may also lead management to delay the recognition of losses, overstate the recoverability of assets, or rely on optimistic assumptions about future performance. Industry instability is particularly relevant when competitors are failing, prices are falling rapidly, financing is tightening, or customer behavior is changing in ways that threaten the entity's business model. Auditors should assess whether management's financial reporting reflects these realities consistently. If reported results appear disconnected from industry conditions, the auditor should consider whether the entity's accounting judgments are masking underlying difficulties.

These entity-level red flags are important because they rarely affect just one account or one disclosure. Instead, they influence the overall environment in which judgments are made, controls are applied, and financial results are communicated. Rapid growth, unusual profitability, financial pressure, structural complexity, related-party influence, leadership instability, and adverse industry conditions each increase the risk that financial reporting may be biased, incomplete, or unreliable. For auditors, recognizing these conditions early helps shape the entire audit strategy. It informs risk assessment, guides planning discussions, and encourages a more skeptical evaluation of management's explanations. A strong entity-level assessment allows the auditor to see the broader forces that may be driving red flags throughout the engagement, making it easier to connect isolated warning signs into a coherent view of audit risk.

Revenue Recognition Red Flags

Revenue recognition is one of the most important and sensitive areas in a financial statement audit, because it directly affects reported earnings, trend analysis, compensation metrics, debt covenant compliance, and investor perceptions. It is also one of the areas most vulnerable to manipulation. Management may face strong incentives to accelerate revenue, smooth results, meet forecasts, or conceal slowing demand, and those incentives can lead to accounting treatments that do not reflect the underlying economics of customer transactions. For auditors, revenue recognition red flags deserve close attention because they often indicate not just isolated transaction errors, but broader problems involving management bias, control weaknesses, or intentional misstatements. A proper audit approach requires understanding how revenue is generated, what contractual terms govern customer arrangements, how performance obligations are satisfied, and whether the timing and amount of recorded revenue are supported by persuasive evidence. When unusual conditions arise, the auditor must determine whether they reflect legitimate business activity or an effort to recognize revenue improperly.

One of the most common red flags is an unusual spike in end-of-period sales. A sharp increase in sales during the final days of a month, quarter, or year does not automatically indicate a problem, since some businesses naturally experience seasonal or cyclical surges. However, when the timing or magnitude of the increase is inconsistent with normal patterns, the auditor should investigate carefully. End-of-period spikes can indicate that management pushed to record transactions before the reporting date in order to meet internal targets or external expectations. The risk is heightened when the spike is accompanied by weak documentation, rushed shipping activity, large manual adjustments, or a subsequent increase in returns and credit memos. Auditors should compare end-of-period sales trends to prior periods, examine shipping terms, inspect supporting contracts, and test whether revenue was recognized in the correct accounting period. The existence of a late-period sales surge is not sufficient by itself to establish misstatement, but it is a classic warning sign that the cutoff and substance of recorded revenue require closer scrutiny.

Another important red flag involves side agreements and undocumented terms. Formal contracts may appear to support revenue recognition, but the real economics of a transaction can be altered by verbal commitments, email exchanges, or informal understandings that are not reflected in the main agreement. These side arrangements may grant return rights, extended payment terms, price protections, cancellation rights, contingencies tied to resale or financing, or promises of future services that affect whether revenue should be recognized and in what amount. When these terms are not captured in the official documentation, the accounting may overstate the certainty or completeness of the performance already delivered. Auditors should be alert when customers negotiate unusually complex terms, when sales personnel appear to control key communications outside the contract process, or when management resists providing all related correspondence. A transaction that appears complete on paper may not meet the applicable recognition criteria if undisclosed obligations or contingencies remain. For this reason, auditors often need to look beyond the signed agreement and consider the full body of evidence surrounding the arrangement, including emails, amendments, payment behavior, and customer confirmations.

EXAMPLE

In 2019, the SEC alleged that senior executives of MiMedx Group used secret side arrangements with distributors that materially changed the economic terms of reported sales. In one arrangement, the distributor did not have to pay MiMedx until it resold the product, and it was also protected for lost, damaged, or returned goods. According to the SEC, those undisclosed terms meant MiMedx should not have recognized revenue when the product was shipped, because the written contract did not reflect the full arrangement.

On paper, the sale could appear complete, with shipment made and a contract in place. But the side arrangement altered collectability, risk transfer, and the existence of continuing obligations. The SEC alleged that the hidden terms were kept from accountants and auditors, which made the company's recorded revenue misleading.

For an auditor, MiMedx illustrates several red flags: management communications outside the formal contract process, reluctance to provide all related correspondence, distributor terms that differ from standard practice, and payment provisions tied to resale rather than a fixed customer obligation. In that setting, the auditor would need to examine emails, amendments, customer confirmations, and actual payment behavior to determine the true substance of the transaction before accepting revenue recognition.

Channel stuffing is another major revenue recognition red flag. This practice occurs when a company induces distributors, resellers, or other channel partners to accept more product than they can reasonably sell in the near term, usually near period-end, in order to inflate its current-period revenue. The company may offer deep discounts, lenient payment terms, extended return rights, or other incentives to encourage the excess purchases. Although the shipments may be real, the economic substance of the transaction may be questionable if the customer lacks genuine demand, faces little economic risk, or expects that unsold goods can be returned or effectively parked until needed. Channel stuffing often leaves a pattern that becomes visible in both financial and operational data. Warning signs may include large quarter-end shipments to existing distributors, unusual growth in receivables, declining sell-through rates, inventory buildups at customer locations, and elevated returns or concessions after period-end. Auditors should not rely solely on the fact that goods were shipped. They must also consider whether control transferred in a meaningful economic sense and whether the arrangement includes terms that undermine finality.

Bill-and-hold arrangements present another area requiring careful audit attention. In these transactions, the seller invoices the customer and may recognize revenue before physical delivery occurs, while retaining possession of the goods for a period of time. Such arrangements can be legitimate in limited circumstances, but they create obvious risk because the timing of billing and the timing of delivery are separated. A company may use a bill-and-hold structure for valid logistical reasons, such as when the customer requests delayed shipment due to storage limitations or project timing. Even so, revenue recognition is appropriate only if specific criteria are met, including evidence that the arrangement is substantive, that the product is separately identified as belonging to the customer, that it is ready for physical transfer, and that the seller does not retain significant obligations that would make the earnings process incomplete. Auditors should be cautious when these arrangements appear near period-end, when the customer's request for delayed delivery is not well documented, or when inventory records do not clearly distinguish the held goods. A bill-and-hold arrangement can easily be used to accelerate revenue if the company records a sale before control has genuinely passed to the customer.

EXAMPLE

In 2023, the SEC charged Evoqua Water Technologies Corp. and certain former executives with improper revenue recognition tied in part to bill-and-hold transactions. According to the SEC, Evoqua recognized revenue even though the products had not been delivered and the arrangements did not satisfy the criteria required under GAAP for bill-and-hold accounting. The SEC said the company used these transactions to help meet internal growth targets and analyst expectations.

This case shows why auditors must treat bill-and-hold arrangements with caution. On the surface, a company may argue that the customer committed to buy the product and that shipment was delayed for business reasons. But the SEC alleged that Evoqua lacked a valid accounting basis for recognizing some of this revenue before delivery. In that setting, the timing of billing and the timing of transfer of control were not aligned, creating a risk that revenue was accelerated improperly.

For an auditor, the warning signs would include period-end sales pressure, incomplete support for the customer's request to delay shipment, inventory still held by the seller, and memoranda prepared to justify the accounting after the fact. The case illustrates why auditors should inspect delivery terms, inventory records, customer communications, and subsequent shipment evidence before accepting bill-and-hold revenue.

Premature revenue recognition more broadly is one of the most significant threats in this area. It occurs when revenue is recorded before the entity has satisfied the relevant performance obligation or before sufficient certainty exists regarding the transaction price and collectability. This problem can arise in many forms, depending on the business model. A company may record revenue upon signing a contract even though goods have not shipped, recognize service revenue before the services have been performed, accelerate milestone revenue without meeting the actual milestone conditions, or treat consignment-like shipments as completed sales. In more complex arrangements, premature recognition may occur because management identifies performance obligations incorrectly, allocates the transaction price inappropriately, or assumes the transfer of control earlier than the contractual and operational facts support. Auditors must therefore understand not only the general accounting framework, but also the mechanics of how the company's products and services are delivered, accepted, and paid for. The risk of premature recognition is especially high where management compensation depends on revenue growth, where estimates and judgment are significant, or where the company operates in industries with customized contracts, software implementation, long-term service obligations, or bundled deliverables. A skeptical auditor will examine whether recorded revenue aligns with actual performance rather than with management's preferred reporting outcome.

Fictitious sales transactions represent a more direct and intentional form of revenue fraud. In these cases, the company records revenue for transactions that never occurred or that lack economic substance. This may involve creating false invoices, fabricating customer accounts, recording shipments that were never made, or recognizing reciprocal or circular transactions designed to simulate legitimate sales activity. Fictitious sales often require supporting falsification in receivables, inventory, shipping documentation, and customer records, especially if the fraud continues over more than one reporting period. Auditors should watch for warning signs such as missing or inconsistent supporting documents, customer confirmations that do not match the books, invoices without valid purchase orders, shipping records with unusual gaps, or sales recorded to unfamiliar customers with little business history. Other indicators may include large sales near period-end followed by no subsequent cash collection, round-dollar invoices, or transactions with entities that appear to have weak commercial substance. Because fictitious sales can be carefully concealed, the auditor must place appropriate weight on third-party evidence, subsequent cash receipts, proof of delivery, and customer existence. When inconsistencies appear in multiple forms of evidence, the possibility of fabricated revenue should be considered directly rather than rationalized away.

EXAMPLE

The SEC found that Centennial Technologies, Inc. improperly recognized revenue from sales where the customer had no real obligation to pay, from sales involving phony product shipments, and from sales where no product was shipped at all. In one striking example, Centennial recorded $1.6 million of revenue from sales of a product called "Flash 98" even though the product did not actually exist.

This is a clear case of fictitious sales revenue. The problem was not merely early recognition or a disputed accounting estimate. The recorded sales lacked genuine economic substance because the underlying transactions were fabricated or fundamentally incomplete. For an auditor, this kind of fraud creates inconsistencies across several categories of evidence at once. If sales are fictitious, receivables may remain unpaid, shipping support may be false or missing, customer obligations may be unclear, and inventory records may not align with what the books claim was sold.

The audit red flags in a case like Centennial would include invoices unsupported by valid purchase commitments, proof of delivery that does not hold up, unusual period-end sales activity, and a lack of subsequent cash collections. When multiple pieces of evidence conflict, the auditor should consider fabricated revenue directly instead of assuming the differences are simple clerical mistakes.

Unusual returns, credits, and allowances are also important red flags because they may reveal that previously recognized revenue was not as final or valid as originally presented. A company may record strong current-period sales only to issue significant credits, discounts, rebates, or returns in the following period. This pattern may indicate aggressive cutoff, channel stuffing, side agreements, or the booking of sales with unresolved contingencies. It can also suggest that the company underestimated variable consideration, failed to establish adequate refund liabilities, or recognized revenue despite a known risk that customers would not retain the product at the stated price. Auditors should evaluate whether post-period concessions are isolated and commercially justified or whether they form a recurring pattern linked to the closing process. A large wave of returns immediately after year-end, especially involving the same customers or products tied to quarter-end sales pushes, may cast doubt on the validity of the earlier revenue recognition. Credit memos and allowances can be especially revealing because they often expose the real terms of transactions that formal contracts failed to capture.

Revenue recognition red flags often do not appear in isolation. A company experiencing an end-of-period sales spike may also show elevated receivables, unusual credit activity after period-end, and incomplete documentation of contract modifications. Side agreements may coexist with channel stuffing. Bill-and-hold arrangements may accompany premature recognition. Fictitious sales may eventually surface through failed confirmations or missing collections. For that reason, auditors should evaluate these warning signs collectively rather than separately. The goal is not merely to identify unusual transactions, but to understand whether the pattern of evidence suggests that reported revenue reflects genuine completed performance or a distorted effort to improve financial results.

Because revenue is so central to performance reporting, even relatively subtle red flags can have significant implications. An auditor who responds effectively to revenue recognition risks must combine technical accounting knowledge with careful contract analysis, data review, cutoff testing, and professional skepticism. The existence of a plausible explanation is not enough. The explanation must be supported by evidence consistent with the substance of the transaction. By recognizing unusual sales patterns, incomplete contractual terms, distribution anomalies, questionable holding arrangements, accelerated recognition practices, fabricated transactions, and post-period concessions, the auditor is better positioned to determine whether revenue has been recorded faithfully. In that sense, revenue recognition red flags are not just isolated audit concerns. They are among the most important signals of whether financial reporting can be trusted.

Cash and Treasury Red Flags

Cash is the most liquid and accessible asset an organization controls, which makes it one of the areas most vulnerable to error, misappropriation, and concealment. Treasury activities also affect borrowing, disbursements, transfers, reconciliations, and short-term liquidity management, so weaknesses in this area can have implications that reach far beyond the cash balance itself. For auditors, cash and treasury red flags are especially important because they often provide early evidence of control failure, financial pressure, or intentional manipulation. A company may appear financially stable on the surface while underlying cash practices reveal operational disorder or fraud risk. Red flags involving cash deserve prompt attention because cash-related irregularities are often easier to conceal in the short term than to sustain over a longer period. The auditor should therefore evaluate not only whether the cash balance is mathematically correct, but also whether the surrounding treasury processes reflect discipline, authorization, transparency, and reliable control.

One of the most basic but important warning signs is the presence of unreconciled bank accounts. Bank reconciliations are a core control because they identify timing differences, recording errors, unauthorized transactions, and unresolved discrepancies between the entity's books and the bank's records. When reconciliations are late, incomplete, or filled with old unreconciled items, the auditor should view that condition as a serious red flag. In some cases, unreconciled differences result from weak staffing, poor training, or disorganized processes. In other cases, they may indicate more serious problems, such as concealed theft, unsupported journal entries, or attempts to delay the recognition of disbursements or shortages. Auditors should pay particular attention to reconciling items that remain outstanding for long periods, are described vaguely, or appear to reverse without clear explanation. The absence of timely reconciliations reduces the entity's ability to detect errors internally and increases the risk that cash-related misstatements can remain undetected through period-end.

Delayed deposits and unusual transfers are also important indicators of risk. A healthy treasury process normally involves the prompt deposit of receipts and routine transfers supported by clear business purposes. When deposits are held for unusual periods, the auditor should consider whether cash is being diverted, whether receipts are being used temporarily for unauthorized purposes, or whether operational controls over collections are weak. Unusual transfers between bank accounts may also suggest efforts to manage appearances rather than reflect actual cash availability. Repeated transfers near period-end, especially if they move between accounts without an obvious operational purpose, can be signs of concealment, temporary window dressing, or efforts to cover shortages. The auditor should examine the timing, frequency, and rationale for such movements of cash. Transfers that occur late in the day, reverse shortly after period-end, or pass through multiple accounts may warrant expanded testing. Treasury movements should make sense in relation to the company's operating pattern, and when they do not, the auditor should investigate further rather than assume a routine explanation.

Frequent manual journal entries involving cash are another significant red flag because cash transactions are usually supported by external evidence and system-generated records. Although some manual entries are legitimate, repeated adjustments to cash accounts, especially near period-end, can indicate that management or accounting personnel are using journal entries to force balances to fit expectations rather than reflect underlying reality. This risk is especially high when entries are posted by senior personnel, lack adequate descriptions, or are unsupported by bank records or other independent documentation. Manual entries may be used to reclassify cash, defer the recognition of disbursements, record unsupported transfers, or conceal shortages through temporary offsets. Auditors should review who posted the entries, when they were posted, what accounts were affected, and whether the explanations are consistent with the business purpose. Patterns matter. A single unusual entry may have a valid explanation, but repeated late-period entries to cash or treasury accounts can point to deeper weaknesses in control or deliberate manipulation. Because cash is normally one of the easiest balances to confirm externally, unexplained manual intervention is inherently suspicious.

EXAMPLE

At the end of the fiscal year, the controller of a manufacturing company realizes that the cash balance shown in the general ledger is lower than the amount management expected to report to its lender. The company is close to violating a loan covenant tied to minimum liquidity levels, and senior management is under pressure to present stronger year-end financial statements. Two days before year-end, the controller posts a manual journal entry debiting cash and crediting an account labeled "intercompany clearing," even though no actual funds were transferred into the bank account. The entry description is vague and states only "year-end adjustment."

A week later, after the financial statements are issued, the controller reverses the entry and replaces it with several smaller manual postings that move amounts among cash, prepaid expenses, and miscellaneous receivables. None of these entries is supported by bank confirmations, transfer documentation, or approved reconciliations.

When the auditor reviews the cash account, the bank confirmation does not match the ledger balance at year-end. Further investigation shows a pattern of similar manual entries at prior quarter-ends. This pattern suggests that management was not correcting legitimate timing issues, but was instead using unsupported journal entries to inflate reported cash and conceal liquidity problems.

Missing supporting documentation is a further warning sign that can undermine confidence in treasury activity. Cash receipts, transfers, disbursements, borrowing arrangements, and investment activity should generally leave a clear paper or electronic trail. When documentation is missing, incomplete, altered, or inconsistent, the auditor should consider whether the transaction was unauthorized, incorrectly recorded, or intentionally obscured. A lack of support may arise from disorganization, but it may also indicate the concealment of improper activity. For example, a disbursement without an approved invoice, a transfer without internal authorization, or a journal entry without bank support weakens the reliability of the recorded transaction. Auditors should be especially alert when missing documentation occurs in clusters, affects unusual items, or coincides with month-end or year-end activity. In treasury functions, documentation is not merely administrative support. It is often the principal evidence that a transaction actually occurred, was properly approved, and was recorded in the right amount and period. When that support is absent, the risk of misstatement rises significantly.

Unauthorized disbursements represent one of the clearest fraud-related risks in the cash cycle. These may take many forms, including payments to fictitious vendors, duplicate payments, altered payees, improper wire transfers, personal expenses charged to the business, or checks issued outside the normal approval process. Unauthorized disbursements often occur where duties are poorly segregated, access to banking platforms is not tightly controlled, or approval procedures can be bypassed by trusted employees or senior managers. They may also be concealed through vague account coding, fabricated supporting documents, or the manipulation of vendor master files. Auditors should evaluate not only whether disbursements are recorded, but whether they were properly authorized, supported, and directed to legitimate recipients for valid business purposes. Warning signs include payments just below approval thresholds, round-dollar wires, weekend or after-hours payment activity, changes to vendor banking instructions without independent verification, or disbursements to unfamiliar counterparties. The presence of unauthorized payments may indicate both direct financial loss and broader control weaknesses that affect other areas of the audit.

Kiting and lapping are more specific schemes, but they remain classic indicators of cash misappropriation and concealment. Kiting involves exploiting timing differences between bank accounts by recording transfers in a way that overstates cash at period-end. A company or individual may record the deposit in one account before recording the corresponding withdrawal from another, causing cash to appear higher than it really is. This is especially relevant when transfers occur near the reporting date and are recorded inconsistently across accounts. Lapping, by contrast, usually involves stealing customer payments and covering the theft by applying subsequent receipts from other customers to the earlier stolen balances. This creates a rolling concealment that can continue for some time if controls over cash receipts and accounts receivable are weak. Red flags include customer complaints about balances already paid, frequent delays in posting receipts, unexplained account adjustments, and unusual timing differences between deposit dates and posting dates. Both kiting and lapping rely on timing manipulation, which means that auditors should pay close attention to cutoff, transfer schedules, deposit records, and the sequencing of receipt applications.

EXAMPLE

Near the end of the year, the assistant treasurer of a wholesale distributor sees that the company's cash balance is lower than expected and worries that management will miss an internal liquidity target. On December 31, she initiates a transfer of $450,000 from Bank A to Bank B. Before the withdrawal clears Bank A, she records the deposit in Bank B on December 31 and includes it in the year-end cash balance. However, she does not record the reduction in Bank A until January 2, when the check or transfer notice clears that account.

As a result, both bank accounts appear to contain the same $450,000 at year-end. The general ledger shows the full balance in Bank A plus the added amount in Bank B, even though only one pool of cash actually exists. This timing difference temporarily inflates total cash and makes the company appear more liquid than it really is.

When the auditor performs a bank transfer schedule, the problem becomes visible. The recorded receipt date in Bank B falls in December, but the recorded disbursement date from Bank A falls in January. The supporting documents show that the transfer was in transit, not additional cash. Because the transaction straddled the reporting date and was recorded inconsistently, the company overstated its year-end cash.

Cash and treasury red flags often reveal more than isolated cash problems. They may signal financial stress, weak supervision, poor systems, inadequate staffing, or intentional fraud. Unreconciled accounts, delayed deposits, unusual transfers, manual cash entries, missing support, unauthorized disbursements, and timing-based concealment schemes all suggest that the organization may not have effective control over its most liquid asset. For auditors, these conditions warrant heightened skepticism and a more focused audit response. Because cash is central to liquidity, solvency, and operational integrity, weaknesses in this area can have consequences that extend across the financial statements. An auditor who evaluates cash and treasury red flags carefully is often in a strong position to detect broader control failures and financial reporting risks before they become harder to unravel.

Receivables Red Flags

Accounts receivable are closely tied to revenue recognition, cash flow, credit risk, and the overall quality of reported earnings. Because receivables represent amounts the company expects to collect from customers, they can easily appear stronger on paper than they are in economic reality. A receivable balance may be overstated because revenue was recognized too early, because customers cannot or will not pay, because credits and concessions have not yet been recorded, or because the balance relates to unusual parties or transactions that do not reflect normal business activity. For auditors, receivables red flags are important because they often reveal problems that extend beyond collection risk alone. They may indicate weaknesses in cutoff, valuation, existence, or disclosure, and they may also point to broader issues involving management bias or fraud. A strong receivables audit therefore requires more than verifying arithmetic accuracy. It requires evaluating whether the recorded balances are legitimate, collectible, properly classified, and supported by the actual economics of customer relationships.

One of the most common red flags is an aging schedule containing large overdue balances. The aging report is a key tool because it shows how long receivables have remained unpaid and highlights concentrations in delinquent categories. A growing volume of balances that are significantly past due may indicate deteriorating customer credit quality, ineffective collection efforts, or the possibility that some recorded receivables are not valid at all. In some cases, old balances remain on the books because management is reluctant to record bad debt expense or write off uncollectible accounts. In other cases, the overdue amounts may reflect unresolved disputes, hidden concessions, or revenue that should not have been recognized in the first place. Auditors should look closely at whether aging categories are consistent with prior periods, whether old balances continue to roll forward without meaningful collection activity, and whether management's allowance for doubtful accounts appropriately reflects the condition of the receivables portfolio. Long-outstanding balances are often more than a credit issue. They can be a warning sign that reported revenue and net receivables are overstated.

Another important red flag is unusual growth in receivables relative to sales. If revenue increases modestly while receivables rise much faster, the auditor should consider whether the company is extending looser credit terms, experiencing collection problems, or recording sales that are not converting into cash as expected. This relationship can be especially revealing when the increase occurs near period-end or when days sales outstanding rise sharply without a clear operational explanation. A mismatch between sales growth and receivables growth may signal aggressive revenue recognition, side agreements affecting payment terms, or slowing customer demand masked by booking more shipments on credit. Auditors should compare receivables turnover trends, examine subsequent cash collections, and evaluate whether payment patterns align with contractual terms and historical experience. The key issue is whether the receivables balance reflects normal business expansion or whether it suggests that recorded revenue is outrunning the company's actual ability to collect from customers.

EXAMPLE

A medical equipment supplier reports that annual sales increased by eight percent, which appears consistent with prior years and with general market conditions. However, its year-end accounts receivable balance rises by 32 percent, and days sales outstanding increase from 54 days to 78 days. Management explains that the increase is caused by "temporary customer delays," but provides little supporting detail. Most of the growth in receivables occurred during the final six weeks of the year, when the company pushed a large volume of product to distributors.

During the audit, several warning signs emerge. Some customers received extended payment terms that were not reflected in the standard sales contracts. In other cases, side emails show that distributors were allowed to return unsold goods after year-end or delay payment until they resold the products. Even though these terms weakened the company's right to immediate payment, the full amount was recorded as current-period revenue.

When the auditor reviews subsequent cash receipts, many of the largest year-end invoices remain unpaid well beyond normal collection periods. A few customers also dispute the recorded amounts, claiming that they had not accepted final delivery terms. The mismatch between modest sales growth and rapid receivables growth suggests that revenue was being recognized faster than cash realization justified. In this case, the receivables balance is not just a byproduct of expansion, but a signal of aggressive revenue recognition and questionable collectability.

Disputed customer balances are another significant red flag because they directly challenge the validity or amount of recorded receivables. A customer may dispute a balance because goods were not delivered as promised, product quality was deficient, contract terms were misunderstood, pricing was incorrect, or promised services were not completed. When disputes exist, the risk is not limited to delayed cash collection.

The underlying issue may mean that revenue should be reduced, deferred, or reversed. Auditors should be cautious when management characterizes disputes as temporary or insignificant without persuasive evidence. Customer complaints, correspondence, legal claims, and unresolved account notes can all provide insight into whether receivables are impaired or whether prior revenue recognition was flawed. Disputes are especially important when they involve large individual customers, transactions recorded near period-end, or recurring issues with the same type of arrangement. A receivable subject to genuine dispute may not meet the assumptions of collectability and finality that supported its original recognition.

Excessive credit memos after period-end can also be a strong indicator of receivables and revenue problems. Credit memos are not unusual in normal operations, since companies may issue them for returns, pricing adjustments, rebates, or billing corrections. However, when large or numerous credit memos are issued shortly after the reporting date, the auditor should consider whether they are effectively reversing sales that should not have been recognized as completed revenue in the first place. This pattern may indicate improper cutoff, channel stuffing, the shipment of unordered goods, undisclosed return rights, or pressure to inflate sales before period-end. Post-period credits can be especially revealing because they show how the company resolves transactions once reporting pressure has passed. Auditors should analyze the timing, cause, customer concentration, and magnitude of credit memos issued after year-end, and determine whether they relate to sales recorded in the period under audit. A surge in post-period credits may undermine the reliability of both receivables and reported revenue.

Weak collection history is another important red flag because it affects the valuation of receivables and may reveal deeper operational or reporting issues. If customers routinely pay late, if collection efforts are inconsistent, or if cash receipts fall well below expectations, management's estimate of net realizable value may be too optimistic. Weak collection history may be caused by declining customer quality, weak credit approval practices, economic stress, or ineffective follow-up by the company. It may also reflect that recorded sales were never strong claims to cash in the first place. Auditors should evaluate collection patterns across customer groups, compare current performance to prior periods, and review subsequent receipts after the reporting date. The quality of collections often provides stronger evidence than management's verbal assurances about customer relationships. A company that continues to report strong receivables while struggling to collect them may be delaying recognition of credit losses or using accounting estimates to preserve earnings. Where collection history is weak, the allowance for doubtful accounts deserves especially careful review.

EXAMPLE

A commercial office furniture distributor reports a strong year-end receivables balance and only a small increase in its allowance for doubtful accounts. Management states that most customers are reliable and that collections will improve in the next quarter. However, the aging report shows that a growing share of receivables is more than 90 days past due, and several long-outstanding balances remain on the books with little documented collection activity. Despite this pattern, the company continues to classify most of the receivables as fully collectible.

During the audit, the auditor reviews subsequent cash receipts and finds that many of the older invoices were still unpaid six weeks after year-end. Some customers have made only partial payments, while others have stopped responding to collection calls altogether. Internal emails reveal that the credit department has repeatedly warned management about deteriorating customer quality, but the sales staff continued shipping products to those customers in order to maintain revenue levels. Collection notes are incomplete, and there is no consistent process for escalating delinquent accounts.

Management argues that the customers are simply experiencing temporary cash flow issues, but the evidence suggests a broader pattern of weak credit oversight and poor collectability. In this situation, the problem is not just slow payment. The company's weak collection history indicates that the recorded receivables may be overstated and that the allowance for doubtful accounts is likely too low.

Related-party receivables concerns present a different but equally important set of risks. Receivables from owners, affiliates, executives, or entities under common control may not behave like ordinary trade receivables, even if they are presented in a similar way. These balances may lack normal credit terms, may not be settled on a timely basis, or may arise from transactions that do not reflect arm's-length economics. In some cases, related-party receivables are used to move profits, support artificial sales growth, or provide indirect financing to affiliated parties without clear disclosure. Auditors should examine whether related-party balances are properly identified, separately disclosed when required, and supported by formal agreements and realistic repayment expectations. Warning signs include vague explanations for the balance, repeated rollovers without payment, nonstandard terms, or settlement through unusual offsets rather than cash. Because related-party transactions may be influenced by motives other than ordinary business considerations, receivables involving such parties require a higher level of skepticism and closer analysis of substance over form.

Receivables red flags are especially valuable to auditors because they often connect several financial statement assertions at once. An old or disputed balance may indicate valuation issues, but it may also signal that the underlying sale lacked substance or that cutoff was improper. Excessive credit memos may point to collectability concerns, but they may also reveal aggressive revenue recognition. Weak collections may reflect customer distress, but they may also expose management's unwillingness to record losses promptly. Related-party balances may seem collectible on paper while masking disclosure or substance issues. For that reason, auditors should evaluate receivables not as isolated numbers but as evidence of how the company records, monitors, and converts revenue into cash.

Inventory Red Flags

Inventory is often one of the most significant and judgment-sensitive asset balances in the financial statements. It affects not only the statement of financial position, but also the cost of goods sold, gross margin, working capital measures, and in some cases impairment or lower-of-cost-and-net-realizable-value assessments. Because inventory typically involves large transaction volumes, physical movement, multiple locations, and valuation judgments, it is highly susceptible to both error and manipulation. For auditors, inventory red flags deserve careful attention because problems in this area can indicate weak operational discipline, ineffective internal controls, or intentional efforts to distort earnings. Inventory irregularities may overstate assets, understate expenses, conceal theft, or mask declining demand. A proper audit approach therefore requires more than verifying counts. It requires understanding how inventory is recorded, moved, safeguarded, valued, and reconciled to the accounting records. When warning signs arise, the auditor should consider whether they reflect routine process problems or conditions that increase the risk of material misstatement.

One classic warning sign is the presence of negative inventory balances in the perpetual records. In some systems, temporary negative balances can arise from timing differences, such as when shipments are recorded before receipts are entered or when system interfaces process transactions out of sequence. Even so, persistent or frequent negative balances are a red flag because they indicate that the inventory records may not accurately reflect what the company actually has on hand. Negative quantities can distort costing calculations, hide cutoff problems, and create opportunities for unsupported adjustments. They may also suggest that management or staff are relying on inaccurate system data to make purchasing, production, and financial reporting decisions. Auditors should evaluate whether negative balances are isolated and promptly resolved or whether they occur repeatedly in specific product lines, locations, or periods. Recurring negatives may point to weak transaction processing, poor supervision, or more serious efforts to manage reported results through improper entries.

Unusual inventory adjustments are another important red flag. Inventory systems often require adjustments for count corrections, damaged goods, production variances, scrap, or unit-of-measure errors. However, when adjustments become frequent, large, round-numbered, or concentrated near period-end, the auditor should investigate whether they are supported and reasonable. Adjustments can be used legitimately to correct errors, but they can also be used to inflate inventory, reduce the cost of sales, or conceal shrinkage. The risk becomes greater when the entries are poorly described, lack independent approval, or are posted manually by a small number of individuals with broad system access. Auditors should pay close attention to the nature of the adjustments, the timing of the postings, the employees involved, and whether the explanations align with the underlying business process. A company that repeatedly relies on large or unexplained inventory entries may not have reliable underlying records, and that condition raises questions about both existence and valuation.

Slow-moving or obsolete inventory is a major red flag because it directly affects the valuation assertion. A company may physically possess inventory that can no longer be sold at normal prices, can only be sold at a discount, or may not be saleable at all. This situation commonly arises when demand declines, products are replaced by newer models, customer preferences change, production specifications shift, or inventory has been held too long relative to its useful selling life. Management may resist writing down obsolete items because doing so reduces current earnings, especially when margins are under pressure. As a result, the balance sheet may continue to reflect historical cost even though the economic value of the inventory has fallen materially. Auditors should examine turnover reports, aging analyses, reserve methodologies, production history, and post-year-end sales activity to determine whether the inventory is realistically valued. Warning signs include stock that has not moved for long periods, items stored in unusual locations, repeated transfers between warehouses, or reserves that remain unchanged despite deteriorating market conditions. Slow-moving inventory is often one of the clearest signals that reported assets may be overstated.

EXAMPLE

An electronics retailer ends the year with a large inventory balance that includes thousands of tablet accessories designed for an older model. The accessories were purchased at full cost six months earlier, when management expected strong holiday demand. However, a newer version of the tablet was released before the holiday season, and customer demand for the older accessories dropped sharply. By year-end, most of the items remain unsold in the warehouse, yet the company continues to carry them at original cost.

Management argues that the products will eventually sell through promotional campaigns, so it records only a minimal inventory reserve. The inventory aging report shows that the affected items have not moved in more than 120 days, and turnover has declined significantly compared with prior periods. The auditor also notices that some boxes of the same products have been transferred repeatedly between store locations and a remote storage site, creating the appearance of activity without actual sales.

When the auditor reviews post-year-end transactions, many of the items are sold only through clearance channels at steep discounts, while others remain unsold altogether. Current selling prices are well below recorded cost, and some products are no longer displayed in regular retail locations. These facts indicate that the inventory is not worth its historical carrying amount. In this case, the slow-moving stock is a clear sign that inventory is overstated and that a larger write-down for obsolescence is necessary.

Inventory held at third-party locations introduces additional risk because the entity does not have direct physical custody of the goods. Inventory may be stored in public warehouses, consignment locations, outside processors, distribution centers, or customer facilities pending use or sale. These arrangements are common in many industries, but they complicate the audit because the auditor cannot simply rely on the company's internal records to establish existence and condition. The risk is heightened when the third-party inventory is significant, spread across multiple locations, or subject to unusual contract terms. Problems may arise if the entity includes goods it does not legally own, fails to include goods it does own, or cannot demonstrate the condition and salability of the items being stored elsewhere. Auditors should examine storage agreements, confirmations from the custodians, shipping records, insurance coverage, and evidence of ownership. They should also consider whether management has clear and timely information about these holdings or whether the balances are carried forward with limited verification. Inventory outside the company's own premises can be legitimate, but it often requires more persuasive audit evidence than on-site holdings.

Large variances between physical counts and book records are another serious warning sign. Some differences are expected in any inventory system due to handling issues, timing differences, measurement errors, or routine shrinkage. However, when the variances are large, repeated, or concentrated in particular products or locations, the auditor should consider whether the perpetual records are unreliable or whether theft, misclassification, or intentional manipulation may be present. Significant count-to-book differences can undermine confidence in both existence and completeness. They may indicate that receipts, issues, transfers, or adjustments are not being recorded properly, or that staff are bypassing established procedures. Auditors should evaluate not only the dollar amount of the variances, but also how management investigates and resolves them. A company with a disciplined control environment will analyze count discrepancies, identify root causes, and implement corrective action. A company that simply posts broad adjustments to absorb the differences without understanding them creates a much higher risk that inventory and the cost of sales are misstated. Physical count problems are especially important when they occur near year-end, because they may directly affect the reported financial statements.

Cutoff problems in shipping and receiving also create important inventory risks. Inventory accounting depends heavily on whether goods in transit, goods received, and goods shipped are recorded in the correct accounting period. If purchases are recorded before the company obtains control of the goods, inventory and liabilities may be overstated. If receipts are delayed in the records, inventory and payables may be understated. On the outbound side, if goods are removed from inventory before the sale is complete or if sales are recorded before control transfers, both inventory and revenue may be misstated. These issues are especially common near period-end, when reporting pressure may encourage aggressive assumptions about shipment and receipt timing. Auditors should test transactions around the cutoff date by examining receiving reports, bills of lading, shipping terms, vendor invoices, and customer delivery evidence. Cutoff errors may arise from poor coordination between logistics and accounting, but they may also reflect deliberate efforts to improve reported results. Because inventory is closely tied to both purchases and sales, cutoff problems often have consequences across multiple financial statement areas.

EXAMPLE

A food products distributor wants to report stronger year-end results, so management closely monitors transactions recorded during the final week of December. On December 30, the company records a large sale of packaged goods to a retail customer and removes the goods from inventory, even though the shipment remains in the company's warehouse until January 3. Under the shipping terms, control does not pass until the goods are delivered to the customer's distribution center. By recording the transaction in December, the company understates ending inventory and overstates current-period revenue.

At the same time, the company receives several inbound deliveries of canned goods from suppliers on December 29 and 31. Warehouse staff unload and store the goods immediately, but the accounting department does not record the receipts until early January, because the vendor invoices were processed after year-end. As a result, both inventory and accounts payable are understated at December 31.

When the auditor performs cutoff testing, these issues become apparent. Bills of lading, receiving reports, and delivery records show that some outbound shipments were recorded too early, while some inbound receipts were recorded too late. The errors affect inventory, revenue, the cost of goods sold, and payables all at once. In this example, poor cutoff procedures distort multiple accounts and create a misleading picture of the company's year-end operating results and financial position.

Fictitious or duplicated inventory items represent a more direct risk of overstatement. In some cases, inventory records may include items that do not physically exist, that have been counted more than once, or that remain in the system even though they were consumed, sold, or scrapped long ago. This problem may result from poor record maintenance, duplicate item codes, system conversion errors, or deliberately fabricated quantities designed to inflate assets and reduce the cost of goods sold. Fictitious inventory can be difficult to detect if the records appear orderly and if physical verification is weak or poorly supervised. Warning signs include unusually high gross margins, inventory growth without corresponding storage capacity, inconsistent item descriptions, repeated count interruptions, a reluctance to allow full observation, or a pattern of adjustments that always increase quantities. Auditors should use physical observation, test counts, location tracing, and system analysis to determine whether recorded items actually exist and are unique. Duplicate or ghost inventory records may seem like a technical system problem, but they can produce material misstatements if left unresolved.

EXAMPLE

A specialty parts manufacturer reports a sharp increase in inventory at year-end, even though production levels and warehouse space have remained relatively stable. Management explains that the increase is due to stronger purchasing efficiency and improved stock availability. However, the auditor notices that gross margins have also risen unexpectedly, even though sales prices have not changed much. This combination raises concern that inventory may be overstated.

During the physical inventory observation, the auditor finds several suspicious conditions. In one warehouse aisle, the same boxes of components appear to be tagged under two different item codes. In the inventory system, one code describes the items as "precision valve assemblies," while another lists nearly identical quantities as "custom flow control units." Further testing shows that the two codes refer to the same physical goods. In addition, some quantities listed in the records cannot be located anywhere in the warehouse, even though they remain on the perpetual inventory report. Production staff later explain that certain items were scrapped months earlier, but the disposals were never recorded.

The auditor also notes that supervisors frequently interrupt the count to discuss adjustments, and most of the post-count changes increase inventory balances. In this case, the company's records include both duplicated items and nonexistent inventory. What appears at first to be a system coding issue is actually causing a material overstatement of inventory and an understatement of the cost of goods sold.

Inventory red flags often appear in combination rather than alone. Negative balances may coexist with unusual adjustments. Slow-moving items may be stored at third-party sites and subject to weak oversight. Large count variances may accompany cut-off errors. Fictitious items may be concealed through repeated manual corrections. For that reason, auditors should assess inventory risks as part of a broader pattern rather than as isolated exceptions. The underlying question is whether the company has a reliable process for recording, safeguarding, counting, and valuing inventory, or whether the reported balance depends too heavily on unsupported assumptions and after-the-fact corrections.

A careful review of inventory red flags helps the auditor evaluate some of the most important financial statement assertions in one of the most risk-prone asset areas. Negative quantities, unexplained adjustments, obsolete stock, third-party custody arrangements, count discrepancies, cutoff weaknesses, and nonexistent items all suggest that the inventory balance may not faithfully represent a company's actual goods or their economic value. When these conditions are present, the auditor should respond with greater skepticism, more extensive testing, and a willingness to challenge management's explanations. In many audits, inventory problems are not limited to warehouse operations. They are signals of broader financial reporting risk, and they deserve correspondingly serious attention.

Fixed Asset Red Flags

Fixed assets often represent a substantial investment by an organization and can affect reported earnings over many periods through depreciation, impairment, maintenance decisions, and disposal accounting. Because these assets are long-lived, capital-intensive, and sometimes operationally dispersed, they are vulnerable to both error and manipulation. Problems in fixed asset accounting may overstate assets, defer expenses improperly, distort depreciation expense, or conceal losses that should already have been recognized. For auditors, fixed asset red flags are important because they often reflect broader weaknesses in capitalization policies, asset tracking, management estimates, and internal controls. A company may appear to have a well-maintained fixed asset schedule, yet the underlying records may contain unsupported additions, assets that no longer exist, or values that no longer reflect economic reality. A sound audit approach therefore requires more than agreeing totals in the ledger. It requires evaluating whether recorded assets exist, are owned by the entity, are properly valued, and continue to provide future economic benefit.

One common red flag is unsupported additions to fixed assets. Capital additions should normally be supported by invoices, contracts, receiving records, internal approvals, and evidence that the asset was placed into service. When significant additions appear without adequate documentation, the auditor should question whether the recorded amounts are valid, complete, and properly classified. Unsupported additions may arise from weak recordkeeping, but they can also indicate efforts to inflate assets or shift expenses out of the current period. The risk becomes greater when additions are recorded through manual journal entries, summarized in vague categories, or posted near period-end without clear operational justification. Auditors should examine whether the asset exists physically, whether the company actually controls it, whether the cost basis is supported, and whether the capitalization date is appropriate. A fixed asset balance that includes undocumented additions is inherently less reliable because the absence of support weakens both the existence and valuation assertions.

Another important red flag is the capitalization of costs that should have been expensed. The distinction between capital expenditures and period expenses is a persistent area of judgment, and management may have incentives to classify ordinary repairs, maintenance, start-up costs, or routine operating expenditures as fixed assets in order to improve current earnings. When this occurs, expenses are deferred improperly and recognized gradually through depreciation rather than immediately in the income statement. Auditors should be especially alert when the company reports unusually strong earnings while capital expenditures rise sharply, or when account descriptions suggest that repair-type activities have been accumulated in asset accounts. For example, roof patching, repainting, equipment servicing, software maintenance, or ordinary replacement parts may not qualify for capitalization unless they clearly extend useful life, increase capacity, or improve efficiency beyond an asset's original standard. The risk is heightened when capitalization policies are vague, thresholds are inconsistently applied, or management pressures the accounting staff to review expenses for items that can be moved to fixed assets. A pattern of aggressive capitalization can materially distort both the balance sheet and operating results.

EXAMPLE

A hotel operator faces rising maintenance costs during the year because several properties require extensive repairs to remain guest-ready. The work includes repainting rooms, replacing worn carpet in hallways, patching sections of roofing, servicing elevators, and repairing aging air-conditioning units. These costs are routine and necessary to keep the buildings in normal operating condition, but they do not materially extend the useful lives of the assets or improve them beyond their original performance standards.

Because management wants to meet an earnings target, the controller directs the accounting staff to charge a large portion of these costs to the fixed asset account called "building improvements" rather than to repairs and maintenance expense. As a result, current-period expenses decline and the reported profit increases. The capitalized amounts are then scheduled for depreciation over several years, even though the underlying work provided little more than short-term upkeep.

During the audit, the auditor reviews additions to fixed assets and notices many invoice descriptions that sound like ordinary maintenance rather than capital improvements. Several invoices refer to patching leaks, repainting guest rooms, and replacing small mechanical parts.

There is no documentation showing that these activities increased capacity, improved efficiency, or extended useful life in a meaningful way.

In this case, management used capitalization to defer normal operating costs. The result is an overstated asset balance, understated expenses, and inflated current earnings.

Missing or idle assets are also significant warning signs. A recorded asset may still appear on the books even though it has been lost, stolen, retired from use, or abandoned. In other cases, an asset may physically exist but no longer contribute meaningfully to operations. Missing assets raise obvious existence concerns, while idle assets raise questions about whether depreciation methods, useful lives, and impairment assessments remain appropriate. Auditors should pay attention when asset tags cannot be located, when departments cannot identify equipment assigned to them, or when facilities contain machinery that appears obsolete, damaged, or unused for long periods. An idle asset is not necessarily impaired, but prolonged nonuse may indicate that the company no longer expects to recover the carrying amount through future operations. A poorly maintained asset register, weak physical verification procedures, and infrequent fixed asset inventories all increase the risk that missing or nonproductive assets remain recorded at values that are no longer supportable.

Unusual depreciation methods or useful lives present another fixed asset red flag. Depreciation should reflect a rational allocation of an asset's cost over the period in which it is expected to provide economic benefit. When management adopts unusually long useful lives, low residual-value assumptions without support, or depreciation methods that do not match the pattern of asset consumption, the resulting expense may be understated. This can improve short-term earnings while leaving asset values higher than they should be. Auditors should compare depreciation policies to industry practice, the nature of the assets, maintenance history, and evidence of actual usage. Sudden changes in useful lives or depreciation methods also deserve close scrutiny, especially when they occur during periods of earnings pressure. While changes in estimates may be legitimate, they should be supported by objective operational facts rather than by a desire to achieve a reporting outcome. Depreciation is often viewed as routine, but it is still based on estimates, and biased estimates can materially affect the financial statements.

Another important warning sign is when impairment indicators are ignored or minimized by management. Fixed assets may be impaired when events or changes in circumstances suggest that their carrying amounts may not be recoverable. Examples include declining demand, plant closures, technological obsolescence, physical damage, regulatory changes, adverse market conditions, or strategic decisions to scale back operations. Management may resist recognizing impairment losses because doing so reduces earnings and may draw attention to unsuccessful investments or deteriorating performance. Auditors should therefore remain alert when there is clear evidence of operational decline but no corresponding discussion of impairment. A facility operating below capacity, equipment tied to discontinued products, or assets affected by significant market changes may warrant formal recoverability testing. Ignoring impairment indicators can overstate both assets and equity, and it may also signal a broader reluctance by management to recognize adverse financial developments promptly.

EXAMPLE

A company that manufactures commercial printing equipment built a specialized production line several years ago to support strong demand for large offset presses. The equipment remains on the books at a high carrying amount, and management continues to depreciate it over its original useful life. During the current year, however, customer demand shifts sharply toward digital printing technology, and sales of the company's traditional presses decline significantly. Production on the older line falls to less than half of normal capacity, and one section of the plant is shut down for extended periods.

Internal reports show that management has scaled back production forecasts, reduced staffing in that area, and begun discussing whether to discontinue one of the related product lines. Even so, no impairment review is performed. Management argues that demand may recover and that the equipment is still technically usable, so it concludes that no further action is needed.

During the audit, the auditor notes several clear impairment indicators: declining cash flows from the product line, underutilized equipment, worsening market conditions, and internal discussions about reducing operations. There is little evidence that the carrying amount of the production line will be recovered through future use. By failing to test the assets for recoverability, management avoids recognizing a likely impairment loss.

In this case, the company's fixed assets and equity are probably overstated. The refusal to address obvious impairment indicators suggests an unwillingness to recognize economic decline on a timely basis.

Inadequate disposal accounting is another red flag in fixed asset auditing. When assets are sold, scrapped, abandoned, or otherwise removed from service, the accounting records should be updated to remove both the asset cost and the related accumulated depreciation, with any resulting gain or loss recognized appropriately. If disposal accounting is weak, the ledger may continue to include assets that are no longer owned or used, and depreciation expense may continue on items that should have been removed. Auditors should look for evidence of assets replaced without corresponding retirements, proceeds from asset sales without disposal entries, or discrepancies between insurance records, maintenance records, and the fixed asset subledger. Inadequate disposal accounting may seem like a housekeeping issue, but over time it can materially distort asset balances and depreciation expense, especially in businesses with frequent equipment turnover.

These fixed asset red flags often appear together. Unsupported additions may coexist with aggressive capitalization. Missing assets may indicate weak tracking and poor disposal procedures. Idle equipment may suggest overlooked impairment and unrealistic useful lives. Inadequate documentation, weak physical controls, and optimistic estimates can combine to produce a fixed asset balance that appears orderly in the accounting records but does not reflect operational reality. For auditors, the key question is whether the fixed asset system captures the full life cycle of an asset accurately, from acquisition through use, impairment, and disposal.

A careful review of fixed asset red flags helps the auditor evaluate existence, valuation, classification, and completeness in an area that can materially affect both the balance sheet and earnings. Unsupported additions, capitalized expenses, missing or idle assets, unusual depreciation assumptions, ignored impairment indicators, and weak disposal accounting all suggest that reported fixed asset amounts may not be reliable. When those conditions are present, the auditor should respond with increased skepticism, deeper testing, and a stronger focus on operational evidence rather than on ledger detail alone.

Liability and Expense Red Flags

Liabilities and expenses are closely linked to the completeness and accuracy of financial reporting, yet they are often more vulnerable to understatement than overstatement. Management that wants to improve reported earnings or strengthen the appearance of liquidity may have an incentive to delay recording obligations, minimize accruals, or classify costs in ways that reduce current-period expense. For auditors, red flags in liabilities and expenses are especially important because they often indicate that the financial statements may omit obligations that already exist or fail to recognize the full cost of operations in the proper period. These issues can affect not only net income, but also working capital, debt covenant compliance, and the reliability of key performance measures. A careful audit approach therefore requires more than reviewing recorded payables and expense accounts. It requires considering what may be missing, understated, or disguised, and whether the entity's processes for identifying obligations are complete and reliable.

One of the most important warning signs is the presence of unrecorded liabilities. A liability may exist even though it has not yet been entered in the accounting system. This often occurs when goods or services have been received before the invoice is processed, when management delays recognizing obligations until cash payment is unavoidable, or when contingent or legal exposures are not properly evaluated. Unrecorded liabilities are particularly significant because they directly affect the completeness assertion. If a company receives inventory before year-end but records the related payable after year-end, both liabilities and expenses may be understated. Similarly, if a service provider completes work before period-end and the company delays accruing the cost, the financial statements will not reflect the true obligations of the business. Auditors should review subsequent disbursements, unmatched receiving reports, vendor statements, unpaid invoices, legal correspondence, and board minutes to identify obligations that existed at the reporting date but were not recorded. The absence of a vendor invoice is not enough to avoid recognition if the company has already incurred the obligation. A pattern of missing liabilities may signal weak cutoff procedures, aggressive earnings management, or a lack of discipline in the closing process.

Expense understatement near period-end is another major red flag because it often reflects deliberate efforts to improve current results. This can occur when management delays recording invoices, defers routine operating costs, reduces accruals without support, or shifts expenses into later periods under the assumption that they can be absorbed when financial pressure eases. The risk is heightened during quarter-end and year-end closing periods, when reporting targets are most visible and small adjustments can have a significant effect on earnings. Auditors should pay attention to unusual drops in expense ratios, unexplained reductions in accrual balances, or post-period invoices that clearly relate to the audited period. Expense understatement may also appear in the form of reclassifications, such as moving ordinary costs into prepaid assets, construction in progress, or other balance sheet accounts without persuasive support. A business does not become more profitable simply because bills are delayed or obligations are ignored. When reported expense levels appear inconsistent with operating activity, staffing levels, production volume, or historical patterns, the auditor should investigate whether the closing process is omitting costs that belong in the current period.

EXAMPLE

At year-end, Ridgewell Distribution was under pressure to meet a lender covenant tied to quarterly earnings. Sales had been flat, freight costs had risen, and management knew that missing the target might trigger difficult discussions with the bank. During the closing process, the controller instructed staff to hold several large vendor invoices in a drawer until early January, even though the related services had been received in December. These invoices included warehouse rent, outside hauling charges, equipment repairs, and utility costs. In addition, the company reduced its accrued bonus and payroll tax liabilities without any documented change in compensation plans or staffing levels. As a further step, a portion of routine maintenance costs for forklifts and loading equipment was reclassified to fixed assets, even though the work merely kept the equipment in normal operating condition.

The result was a noticeable decline in operating expenses and an unexpected improvement in reported profit for the fourth quarter. An auditor comparing monthly expense trends to shipping volume and headcount noticed that December expenses were unusually low despite no decline in activity. Subsequent review of January cash disbursements revealed invoices dated before year-end that related to December operations. The auditor also found unsupported journal entries reducing accruals and shifting ordinary repairs to asset accounts. Together, these items indicated that management had understated expenses to inflate period-end earnings.

Unusual vendor relationships are another important indicator of risk. Not every non-standard vendor arrangement is improper, but certain patterns deserve closer scrutiny because they may conceal undisclosed related parties, conflicts of interest, kickback schemes, or fabricated disbursements. Red flags include vendors with limited business history, vendors sharing addresses or bank accounts with employees or executives, repeated payments to entities with vague service descriptions, or a concentration of purchases routed through one vendor without a clear business reason. Auditors should also be alert when vendor master files change frequently, when supporting documentation is unusually sparse, or when bidding and approval processes appear to have been bypassed. A vendor relationship that lacks transparency can affect both liabilities and expenses. It may lead to fictitious or inflated charges, improper classification of expenditures, or obligations that are structured to conceal their true nature. Reviewing vendor patterns can therefore reveal not only purchasing irregularities but also broader weaknesses in internal control and financial reporting reliability.

EXAMPLE

During the audit of a regional construction supplier, an auditor noticed that payments for "consulting" and "logistics coordination" had increased sharply over the past year. Most of these payments were directed to a little-known vendor called Summit Trade Partners, which had been added to the vendor master file only eight months earlier. The vendor had no meaningful website, no clear operating history, and invoices that contained vague descriptions with no detail about dates, hours worked, or specific deliverables. Further testing showed that the vendor's mailing address matched a property owned by the company's purchasing manager, and the bank account receiving payments had been updated twice in a short period. Despite the volume of payments, there was no evidence that competitive bids had been obtained or that senior management had documented any reason for concentrating work with this vendor.

When the auditor expanded testing, additional concerns emerged. Several invoices had been approved by the same purchasing manager who had requested the work, and supporting documents consisted only of copied invoice covers without contracts or work reports. Some charges had been recorded as operating expenses, while others were capitalized into inventory handling costs without justification. Interviews with warehouse staff suggested that many of the billed services had actually been performed by internal employees. These findings raised the possibility of a related-party arrangement, inflated billings, or fictitious disbursements designed to divert company funds.

Round-dollar or duplicate payments are another classic red flag in the expense cycle. A round-dollar payment is not automatically improper, but repeated round-dollar amounts, especially in areas where invoices would normally vary, can indicate fabricated transactions, manual overrides, or insufficient scrutiny of disbursement activity. Duplicate payments are equally concerning because they may reflect poor invoice matching controls, intentional abuse of the payment system, or efforts to move cash out of the company under the appearance of routine operations. Auditors should review payment files for repeated amounts, closely timed disbursements to the same vendor, invoices with similar numbers or dates, and payments that do not match receiving records or purchase orders. The risk is especially high when the company lacks automated duplicate-check controls or when payment approval authority is concentrated in a small number of individuals. These patterns matter because they may indicate that the company is paying amounts it does not truly owe, or that liabilities and expenses have been manipulated through weak processing controls.

Improper accrual estimates represent another major area of concern. Many liabilities and expenses must be recorded through estimation because the exact amount is not yet known at period-end. Examples include bonuses, warranty obligations, legal exposures, utility costs, vacation pay, incentive compensation, sales returns, and restructuring charges. Estimation is a normal part of financial reporting, but it becomes a red flag when assumptions are overly optimistic, inconsistent with past experience, or changed without clear justification. Management may understate accruals to improve earnings or avoid drawing attention to deteriorating conditions. In other cases, accruals may be manipulated in the opposite direction to create reserves that can be released in future periods. Auditors should evaluate whether the methodology is reasonable, whether assumptions are supported by evidence, and whether the estimate aligns with subsequent outcomes when available. A company that consistently records accruals at the low end of a reasonable range, despite contrary evidence, may be introducing bias into the financial statements. Because accruals often involve judgment rather than direct invoicing, they are a common target for earnings management and deserve a high level of audit skepticism.

EXAMPLE

At year-end, Harbor Home Products faced pressure to report stable earnings despite rising product failures and a costly employee retention program. Management recorded a warranty accrual based on an outdated claim percentage from two years earlier, even though recent service reports showed a sharp increase in returns and repair requests for a newly launched appliance line. At the same time, the company reduced its bonus accrual by assuming that several performance targets would not be met, even though internal forecasts prepared before year-end indicated the targets were likely to be achieved. No clear documentation explained why these assumptions had changed. The combined effect was to reduce current-period expenses and improve reported income.

During the audit, the auditor compared current accrual assumptions to prior-year methods, recent operating data, and subsequent events. Warranty claims filed in the first two months of the new year were significantly higher than the level implied by the recorded reserve. Human resources records and management dashboards also showed that bonus targets had, in fact, been met, making the reduced bonus accrual difficult to support. Further review revealed that management routinely selected assumptions at the low end of a reasonable range, even when contrary evidence suggested a higher estimate was more appropriate. The pattern suggested more than simple estimation error. It indicated possible management bias in accrual accounting, with liabilities and expenses deliberately understated to present stronger year-end results.

Payroll irregularities and ghost employees present another significant risk within liabilities and expenses. Payroll is often one of the largest recurring expense categories in an organization, and weaknesses in payroll processing can affect both wage expense and accrued compensation liabilities. A ghost employee scheme occurs when fictitious or inactive individuals remain in the payroll system and continue to receive payments, often through accounts controlled by the perpetrator. Other payroll red flags include duplicate bank accounts, employees without valid personnel files, unusual overtime patterns, salary changes without authorization, terminated employees still receiving pay, or payroll disbursements that do not reconcile to headcount and labor activity. Payroll fraud can be particularly difficult to detect if human resources, payroll processing, and payment approval are not properly segregated. Auditors should compare payroll records to personnel files, review access rights over payroll master data, test for duplicate addresses or bank accounts, and analyze unusual trends in compensation. Payroll irregularities may indicate direct theft, but they may also reflect weak controls over authorization, accruals, and the classification of labor costs.

These liability and expense red flags often appear together rather than in isolation. Unrecorded liabilities may coincide with understated accruals. Weak vendor controls may lead to duplicate payments or concealed related-party transactions. Payroll irregularities may coexist with deficient approval procedures and poor segregation of duties. Expense understatement near period-end may be reinforced through aggressive estimates or delayed invoice processing. When several of these conditions are present, the risk is not merely that one account is misstated. It is that the entity's broader process for recognizing obligations and recording costs may be unreliable.

A careful review of liabilities and expenses helps the auditor determine whether the financial statements reflect the full cost of doing business and the full amount of obligations incurred as of the reporting date. Unrecorded liabilities, understated expenses, unusual vendor patterns, suspicious payment activity, biased accruals, and payroll anomalies all suggest that the entity may be presenting a more favorable financial picture than the underlying economics support. When these warning signs arise, the auditor should respond with more extensive cutoff testing, stronger corroboration, and a willingness to challenge management's assumptions and explanations. In many audits, the most revealing question is not what has been recorded, but what should have been recorded and was not.

General Ledger Red Flags

The general ledger is the central repository of an organization's accounting activity, and journal entries are the mechanism by which balances are created, adjusted, corrected, and reclassified. Because journal entries can affect nearly any account in the financial statements, they are one of the most important areas for auditors to examine when assessing red flags. Many fraudulent or misleading accounting treatments ultimately flow through journal entries, even when the underlying scheme begins elsewhere. A company may have formal transaction systems for sales, purchasing, payroll, and inventory, but management can still alter reported results through manual postings, unsupported adjustments, and reclassifications that bypass normal processing. For this reason, journal entry testing is a core part of audit work, especially in evaluating management override of controls. Red flags in the general ledger do not automatically prove misconduct, but they often reveal where accounting results may have been shaped by judgment, pressure, or concealment rather than by ordinary business activity.

One of the clearest warning signs is the presence of manual entries posted late in the period. Manual journal entries are not inherently improper, since companies often need them for accruals, corrections, consolidations, and other legitimate purposes. However, entries posted at the end of a month, quarter, or year deserve special attention because they may have a direct effect on reported results at the point when management is under the greatest pressure to meet expectations. A late-period entry that increases revenue, reduces expenses, or shifts balances among key accounts may be entirely valid, but the auditor should evaluate whether it reflects a genuine accounting need or a result-driven adjustment. Timing matters because an entry posted after most routine transaction processing has already occurred can indicate an attempt to change the final picture rather than to record normal activity. Auditors should examine when the entry was posted, who posted it, whether it was reviewed independently, and whether the amount and account combinations make sense in the context of the business. Entries made after normal closing deadlines, on weekends, or immediately before financial statements are finalized may warrant particular scrutiny.

EXAMPLE

At the end of the fiscal year, Meadowline Medical Supply was struggling to meet profit expectations after a surge in employee turnover and product complaints. Management was required to estimate several liabilities, including vacation pay, customer rebate obligations, and a pending legal settlement involving defective equipment. Instead of updating these accruals using current information, the chief financial officer relied on prior-year percentages that no longer reflected actual conditions. Vacation accruals were reduced even though payroll records showed that employees had accumulated more unused leave than in the prior year. Customer rebate expense was held flat despite a sales promotion that significantly increased rebate eligibility. The legal accrual was recorded at a minimal amount, even though outside counsel had advised that a larger settlement range was probable.

The auditor became concerned when these estimates appeared unusually low compared with operating activity and internal records. A review of post-year-end payments showed that rebate claims and vacation payouts were substantially higher than the amounts accrued. Legal correspondence also indicated that management had ignored unfavorable information when selecting its estimate. Further analysis showed a pattern of choosing assumptions that minimized expense recognition without persuasive support. Although each estimate involved judgment, the overall direction of the judgments was consistently favorable to reported earnings. This pattern suggested that the company was not merely making weak estimates, but was using the accrual process to understate liabilities and improve period-end results.

Entries lacking explanations or support are another important red flag. A journal entry should ordinarily include a clear description of its purpose and enough supporting documentation to allow a reviewer to understand why it was recorded. When descriptions are vague, such as "adjustment," "reclass," or "to correct error," and there is no supporting analysis, invoice, schedule, or approval, the reliability of the entry becomes questionable. Unsupported entries may result from weak documentation practices, but they can also be a sign that the adjustment would not withstand closer examination. Auditors should be cautious when entries are large, unusual, or recurring, yet are supported only by spreadsheets prepared internally without corroboration. The lack of support is especially concerning when the entry affects revenue, reserves, liabilities, or other judgment-sensitive areas. An unsupported journal entry undermines auditability because it prevents a clear link between the accounting record and the underlying economic event. Where support is missing, the auditor should not assume that the amount is reasonable simply because it appears in the ledger.

Unusual entries made by senior management represent a particularly significant risk because they may reflect management override of normal controls. Senior executives often have the authority to direct accounting personnel, approve adjustments, or gain access to reporting processes that lower-level employees cannot influence. That authority is not improper in itself, but it becomes a red flag when senior management initiates entries that are unusual in nature, occur outside routine processes, or affect earnings in sensitive periods. For example, a chief financial officer may direct a late reclassification, reserve release, or top-side consolidation entry that changes the reported outcome materially. Because senior personnel are often in a position to override reviews or pressure staff not to question their decisions, entries associated with them deserve heightened skepticism. Auditors should evaluate whether senior management entries are consistent with legitimate oversight responsibilities or whether they appear to bypass established approval channels and accounting logic. The risk is especially high when the entry has no clear operational basis, when employees seem reluctant to explain it, or when similar entries appear repeatedly at reporting dates.

Round-dollar or repetitive entries are also classic warning signs in journal entry analysis. Many ordinary transactions naturally result in uneven amounts based on invoices, payroll calculations, taxes, or system-generated formulas. By contrast, fabricated or management-directed entries often appear in round numbers because they are designed to achieve a target rather than reflect an underlying transaction. A series of entries for amounts such as \$100,000, \$250,000, or \$1,000,000 may suggest that balances are being adjusted to produce a desired financial statement result. Repetition is equally important. If similar entries appear each month or quarter, especially with little variation in amount or explanation, they may indicate routine manipulation, unsupported reserve activity, or an attempt to smooth earnings. Auditors should not treat round numbers as suspicious in every case, since some accruals and allocations are legitimately estimated in broad amounts. Still, when round-dollar entries occur alongside vague descriptions, late posting times, or unusual account pairings, the pattern becomes more significant. Journal entry review is often most effective when the auditor evaluates combinations of risk factors rather than one characteristic in isolation.

Entries posted to seldom-used accounts also deserve close attention. Many organizations have accounts that are rarely used except for highly unusual transactions, legacy balances, or infrequent events. When journal entries begin appearing in these accounts unexpectedly, the auditor should consider whether they are being used to park amounts temporarily, obscure classification issues, or avoid attention from routine financial statement review. A seldom-used account may attract less scrutiny from management and staff, making it a convenient place to record unsupported adjustments. This risk is heightened when the account title is vague, when balances fluctuate sharply near period-end, or when the entry has no obvious relationship to business activity. For example, an account labeled "other assets," "miscellaneous liabilities," or "suspense" can become a repository for unresolved or intentionally hidden items if the closing process is weak. Auditors should review the history, purpose, and normal activity of these accounts and determine whether recent postings are justified by underlying events. A rarely used account is not automatically problematic, but unusual activity in it may signal that management is using the ledger structure itself to reduce visibility.

EXAMPLE

During the audit of North Valley Components, the auditor noticed an unusual year-end increase in an account labeled "Other Deferred Items," which historically had little or no activity. In prior years, the account had been used only for infrequent insurance recoveries and minor timing differences, yet in the final week of the current year several large manual journal entries were posted to it. The entries reduced operating expenses and offset accounts payable, but the descriptions were vague, using phrases such as "reclassification," "year-end adjustment," and "management review entry." No supporting invoices, contracts, or schedules were attached. Because the account was not part of the company's normal monthly review process, these postings had not attracted internal attention.

When the auditor traced the entries, it became clear that routine expenses had been moved out of expense accounts and parked temporarily in this seldom-used asset account. The items included plant maintenance costs, outside service fees, and accrued utility charges that clearly related to the current period. Management claimed that the entries were temporary and would be reversed after additional review, but no evidence suggested that the amounts met the definition of an asset. Further investigation showed that the entries had been posted late in the closing process by a senior accounting manager without secondary approval. The unusual use of a dormant account suggested an attempt to hide expenses and improve reported earnings by placing unsupported amounts where they were less likely to be questioned.

Reclassifications that obscure results are another major journal entry red flag. Reclassification entries can be entirely legitimate, especially in complex organizations where balances must be moved for presentation, consolidation, or correction. However, they can also be used to shift amounts among accounts in ways that make performance appear stronger or risks appear smaller. For example, expenses may be reclassified to assets, operating costs may be moved below the line, short-term liabilities may be shifted into less visible categories, or unusual losses may be offset against unrelated gains. Reclassifications may not change total assets or total net income in every case, but they can still distort key subtotals, ratios, and disclosures relied on by users of the financial statements. Auditors should pay close attention to whether reclassifications have a clear accounting rationale, whether they are consistent from period to period, and whether they affect key performance measures in ways that seem advantageous to management. An entry that improves gross margin, operating income, or working capital without a corresponding business event may be more about presentation management than faithful reporting. Reclassifications can be particularly misleading because they may appear technical and innocuous while materially altering how results are understood.

These journal entry and general ledger red flags often reinforce one another. A late-period manual entry may also be round-dollar, posted by senior management, and recorded in a seldom-used account. An unsupported adjustment may be disguised as a reclassification. Repetitive entries may reveal a pattern of smoothing results over time. For that reason, auditors should assess journal entries holistically rather than viewing each characteristic separately. Modern audit tools often allow large-scale data analysis of entry populations, which can help identify these patterns, but the real value lies in interpreting what the patterns mean in the context of the company's operations, control environment, and reporting pressures.

A careful review of journal entries and the general ledger provides auditors with one of the clearest windows into how reported results were assembled. Manual late-period entries, vague or unsupported postings, senior management adjustments, round-dollar patterns, unusual use of dormant accounts, and reclassifications that alter the appearance of results all suggest that the accounting records may contain more than routine processing. When these warning signs are present, the auditor should respond with heightened skepticism, stronger corroboration, and a focused effort to determine whether the entries reflect legitimate accounting judgments or efforts to manipulate the financial statements.

Estimate and Valuation Red Flags

Estimates and valuation judgments are among the most sensitive areas in a financial statement audit because they often involve uncertainty, management judgment, and assumptions about future events rather than directly observable facts. Unlike a cash balance confirmed by a bank or an invoice matched to a purchase order, many estimated amounts depend on probability assessments, valuation models, historical patterns, market inputs, and management expectations about future performance. These areas create risk because even small changes in assumptions can materially affect reported earnings, asset values, liabilities, and disclosures. They also create opportunity for bias. Management under pressure to meet targets may not need to fabricate transactions if it can instead adjust assumptions in ways that make estimates appear reasonable while still favoring a desired reporting outcome. For auditors, estimate and valuation red flags are especially important because they often reveal whether management is exercising neutral judgment or using estimation flexibility to shape the financial statements.

One major warning sign is the use of biased assumptions in accounting estimates. An estimate may appear technically supportable while still reflecting a one-sided choice of assumptions that consistently favors higher income, stronger asset values, or lower liabilities. Examples include assuming lower default rates in expected credit loss models, selecting optimistic warranty claim patterns, using lower expected return requirements in impairment testing, or choosing assumptions that minimize pension obligations. Bias is often revealed not by one assumption alone, but by a pattern in which management repeatedly selects the most favorable point within a reasonable range. Auditors should compare assumptions to historical experience, current conditions, and external data where available. They should also assess whether management's assumptions are internally consistent across different estimates. For example, a company should not assume a weak economy when justifying one estimate and a strong economy when supporting another, unless there is a clear reason for the difference. Biased assumptions are especially concerning when management cannot explain why certain inputs were chosen or when the assumptions consistently produce results that improve reported performance.

EXAMPLE

At year-end, Crestline Finance was required to estimate its allowance for credit losses on a growing portfolio of customer receivables. Economic conditions in several of its markets had weakened, delinquency trends were rising, and recent collection results had deteriorated. Even so, management used an expected loss model built on unusually low default assumptions and a rapid recovery rate that exceeded both the company's own recent history and broader industry data. Management argued that the portfolio was "high quality," but could not provide persuasive evidence explaining why current-period risks were lower than in prior years. At the same time, the company used very optimistic assumptions in testing a customer-related intangible asset for impairment, including strong future cash flow growth and a low discount rate. In both cases, the selected assumptions reduced expense recognition and supported stronger reported asset values.

The auditor became concerned because the assumptions showed a consistent directional bias. Management assumed fewer customer defaults despite worsening credit trends, yet also assumed strong future demand when defending asset values. These positions were difficult to reconcile with the same external environment. A comparison to historical outcomes showed that prior estimates had also tended to be overly favorable, followed by later adjustments when actual results turned out worse. Although each individual assumption could be described as falling within a broad reasonable range, the repeated selection of the most optimistic inputs suggested management bias. The pattern indicated that estimates were being shaped to improve reported performance rather than reflect neutral judgment.

Unsupported fair value measurements are another significant red flag. Fair value estimates often require valuation models, observable market inputs, appraisals, discounted cash flow analyses, or other specialized methods, depending on the nature of the asset or liability. When fair value measurements are based on weak data, outdated appraisals, internally generated models without validation, or assumptions that are not grounded in market evidence, the reliability of the reported amount becomes questionable. The risk is greatest where inputs are unobservable and management has broad discretion, such as in private company valuations, complex financial instruments, acquired intangible assets, impaired long-lived assets, and certain contingent consideration arrangements. Auditors should be cautious when management relies heavily on third-party valuations without understanding the underlying methods, when model assumptions do not align with market trends, or when values remain unchanged despite obvious shifts in economic conditions. A fair value estimate is not persuasive merely because it was calculated using a sophisticated model. The supporting data, assumptions, and methodology must be relevant, consistent, and defensible. Where those elements are weak, the estimate may be materially misstated even if it appears mathematically precise.

Inconsistent reserve methodologies also deserve attention because consistency is a key feature of reliable estimation. A reserve methodology should be based on a rational approach that is applied consistently over time unless circumstances change in a documented and supportable way. Problems arise when management changes the way it calculates reserves without clear justification, applies different methodologies to similar items, or adjusts methods from one period to the next in a way that consistently improves results. For example, a company may use historical loss trends when those trends produce a lower reserve, then shift to selective current data when that produces an even lower result, without a principled explanation. Inconsistency can also appear when different business units apply varying assumptions to similar risks without any centralized oversight. Auditors should evaluate whether reserve methodologies are documented, whether changes are clearly explained, and whether the methods align with actual loss experience and current conditions. A reserve process that changes opportunistically is a red flag because it suggests that management may be using methodology selection as a tool for earnings management rather than for neutral estimation.

Understated allowances and contingencies represent another major estimate and valuation risk. Many liabilities and contra-asset accounts depend on management's willingness to recognize probable losses or reductions in value before they become certain. Examples include allowances for doubtful accounts, sales returns, inventory obsolescence, warranty obligations, legal contingencies, environmental liabilities, restructuring costs, and self-insurance reserves. These amounts are often vulnerable to understatement because recognizing them reduces current earnings and may draw attention to deteriorating conditions. Auditors should be especially alert when reserves remain flat despite changing business conditions, when contingency disclosures are vague, or when management argues that losses are not probable despite substantial negative evidence. Subsequent events can be particularly useful in evaluating whether a recorded estimate was reasonable at period-end. If the company experiences a wave of returns shortly after year-end, settles litigation for a significant amount, or writes off receivables soon after the reporting date, the auditor should consider whether the earlier estimate was understated. Understated allowances and contingencies often create a falsely favorable picture of both profitability and financial condition, and they are a common area of management bias.

EXAMPLE

At year-end, Silver Ridge Electronics reported strong earnings even though product quality problems and customer payment issues had been mounting for months. The company's allowance for doubtful accounts remained nearly unchanged from the prior year, despite a noticeable increase in slow-paying customers and a rise in past-due balances over 90 days. Management also kept its sales return reserve flat even though a recently introduced product line had generated frequent customer complaints and a growing number of return authorizations. At the same time, the company disclosed a pending lawsuit involving alleged product defects but recorded no meaningful legal accrual, arguing that a loss was only reasonably possible. Internal correspondence from legal counsel, however, suggested that an unfavorable settlement was increasingly likely.

The auditor became concerned because these estimates did not reflect worsening business conditions. A review of events shortly after year-end revealed that several large receivables were written off, customer returns increased sharply, and the lawsuit was settled for a material amount. These outcomes did not prove that management should have predicted the exact amounts, but they did indicate that the year-end estimates had been too low. Further analysis showed that management had relied on outdated reserve percentages and had not incorporated current information from collections staff, product service reports, or legal counsel. The pattern suggested bias rather than simple estimation error. By understating allowances and contingencies, the company had presented higher income, stronger receivables, and fewer liabilities than the circumstances supported.

Overly optimistic forecasts are another important red flag because many valuation models and recoverability analyses depend on management's view of future performance. Forecasts are used in impairment testing, fair value calculations, deferred tax asset realizability assessments, purchase accounting valuations, and going concern evaluations, among other areas. A forecast becomes problematic when it assumes aggressive revenue growth, unrealistic margin improvement, rapid cost reductions, or economic recovery that is not supported by the company's recent history or by market conditions. Management may argue that the forecast reflects strategic plans or expected improvements, but the auditor must determine whether those expectations are grounded in evidence or merely serve to support a preferred accounting conclusion. Auditors should compare current forecasts to prior forecasts and actual outcomes, examine whether the company has historically met its projections, and consider whether external industry data aligns with the assumptions being used. A pattern of missed projections followed by equally aggressive new forecasts is a strong warning sign. Forecasts should be evaluated not only for internal logic, but also for credibility in light of actual performance and the broader environment.

EXAMPLE

At year-end, Horizon Fitness Centers tested the carrying value of several underperforming locations for impairment. Recent results had been weak. Membership growth had stalled, cancellation rates were rising, and several clubs had missed internal profit targets for most of the year. Even so, management prepared a forecast showing a sharp rebound beginning in the first quarter of the next year. The projection assumed double-digit revenue growth, improved retention, significant price increases, and immediate labor savings from a restructuring plan that had not yet been approved. These assumptions allowed management to conclude that the locations would recover their carrying amounts and that no impairment charge was necessary.

The auditor became concerned because the forecast looked much stronger than both recent operating results and prior internal projections. In the preceding two years, management had repeatedly forecasted recoveries that never occurred, yet the new model was even more aggressive. Industry data also showed increasing competitive pressure and slower consumer spending in the company's markets, which did not support the projected rebound. When the auditor asked for evidence, management provided only broad strategic explanations rather than signed contracts, approved cost-reduction plans, or reliable market support. A comparison of forecast assumptions to actual results in the first months of the new year showed that revenue and margins were already falling short. The pattern suggested that the forecast had been built to avoid an impairment loss rather than to present a neutral estimate of future performance.

Changes in assumptions without justification are another significant red flag because they can materially alter reported amounts even when the underlying estimation model stays the same. A company may lower a discount rate, extend an asset's useful life, reduce a loss factor, increase a terminal growth rate, or revise expected claim patterns in a way that improves current-period results. Some changes are entirely appropriate when new information becomes available, but they should be supported by evidence and clearly documented. The concern arises when assumptions change in favorable directions without any corresponding operational, economic, or market development to explain them. Auditors should compare current assumptions to those used in prior periods, identify the effect of the changes, and assess whether management has a persuasive basis for the revision. It is especially concerning when assumptions are adjusted during periods of earnings pressure or when multiple favorable changes occur simultaneously across different estimates. Unjustified assumption changes may indicate that management is fine-tuning results through estimation rather than recognizing the underlying economics of the business.

Estimate and valuation red flags often interact. Biased assumptions may support understated reserves. Unsupported fair value measurements may rely on overly optimistic forecasts. Methodology changes and assumption changes may work together to produce more favorable reported results without a clear external basis. For that reason, auditors should not evaluate each estimate in isolation. They should also consider the broader pattern of management judgment across the financial statements. When several estimates all trend in a favorable direction despite adverse business conditions, the risk of overall management bias becomes much greater.

A careful review of estimate and valuation red flags helps the auditor assess whether judgment has been exercised neutrally or strategically. Biased assumptions, weak fair value support, inconsistent methodologies, understated allowances, optimistic projections, and unsupported changes in assumptions all suggest that estimates may be doing more than reflecting uncertainty. They may be shaping the reported results in a preferred direction. Because estimates often involve complex reasoning and cannot be proven with exact precision, this area requires especially strong professional skepticism. The auditor must look beyond the mechanics of the calculation and evaluate whether the assumptions, methods, and conclusions are credible in the context of the company's actual circumstances. In many audits, the most significant red flags are not found in simple arithmetic errors, but in estimates that appear reasonable only because the underlying optimism has not been challenged carefully enough.

Related Party Red Flags

Related-party transactions are among the most sensitive areas in an audit because they can be used to shift profits, conceal obligations, distort performance, or hide the true nature of business relationships. These transactions are not inherently improper. Many organizations legitimately transact with affiliates, owners, executives, family members, or entities under common control. However, related-party arrangements often carry higher risk because they may not be negotiated on normal commercial terms, may be motivated by objectives other than ordinary business purpose, and may be structured in ways that are less transparent than third-party transactions. For auditors, related-party red flags matter because they affect not only disclosure, but also the substance, valuation, timing, and classification of recorded amounts. A company may report a transaction as though it were a routine sale, loan, or expense, while the underlying relationship changes its economic meaning entirely. Careful attention to related-party indicators is therefore essential to identifying misstatement risk.

One of the most important red flags is the existence of undisclosed related parties. A company may fail to identify an affiliate, a management-controlled entity, a family-linked counterparty, or another party capable of exerting significant influence over its decisions. This omission can occur because management lacks discipline in its disclosure process, but it can also be intentional when the relationship would raise questions about the legitimacy of transactions or the independence of decision making. Auditors should be alert when names recur across contracts, vendor files, customer lists, board minutes, legal documents, or financing arrangements in ways that suggest connections not disclosed formally. Common signs include shared addresses, overlapping officers, common bank contacts, unusually familiar communication patterns, or transactions approved outside normal channels. Undisclosed related parties are especially concerning because they may be involved in revenue transactions, loans, guarantees, service arrangements, or asset transfers that would be viewed differently if users understood the underlying connection. If the auditor does not identify the relationship, it becomes much easier for management to present the transaction as arm's length when it is not.

EXAMPLE

During the audit of Pine Harbor Manufacturing, the auditor noticed repeated sales to a customer called East Ridge Industrial, a company that had become one of Pine Harbor's largest year-end buyers in less than six months. The transactions appeared unusual because the customer placed large round-dollar orders near quarter-end, received extended payment terms, and returned very little communication through the normal sales channel. When the auditor reviewed corporate records and public registration documents, East Ridge's mailing address matched the address of a small office building owned by Pine Harbor's chief executive officer. Further inquiry showed that East Ridge's president was the brother of Pine Harbor's operations vice president, yet no related-party disclosure had been made in the financial statements or board materials.

The concern deepened when the auditor examined how the sales had been approved. The transactions bypassed the company's standard credit review process, and several shipments were authorized directly by senior management. Payment had not yet been received on many of the invoices, but management continued to describe the customer as an independent third party. Additional review of email traffic and contract files showed unusually informal communication and side arrangements involving storage concessions and flexible return rights. If the relationship had been disclosed properly, users might have questioned whether the sales were negotiated on arm's-length terms or whether they were structured to improve reported revenue.

The undisclosed family and management connection suggested that the customer relationship had been intentionally obscured.

Another major red flag is a transaction that lacks economic substance. A related-party arrangement may be documented formally and recorded accurately in a mechanical sense, yet still fail to reflect a genuine business purpose. In these cases, the transaction may exist primarily to create the appearance of revenue, move losses, support asset values, improve liquidity ratios, or shift obligations away from the reporting entity. For example, an affiliate may purchase goods without a realistic intent or ability to use them, a parent may route funds through a subsidiary to make activity appear external, or one commonly controlled entity may sell an asset to another at a contrived value without any real change in economic position. Auditors should evaluate whether the transaction changes the entity's rights, risks, and obligations in a meaningful way, or whether it merely creates accounting consequences without substantive economic change. The existence of a signed agreement is not enough. The arrangement should make sense in light of the parties' operations, financial capacity, and business objectives. A lack of economic substance is one of the strongest indicators that a related-party transaction may be designed to mislead rather than to conduct ordinary business.

EXAMPLE

At year-end, Meridian Office Furnishings sold a large quantity of slow-moving inventory to an affiliated distributor controlled by the chief executive officer's family. The sale was recorded as revenue in the current period, which allowed the company to report stronger earnings and reduce excess inventory balances. On paper, the transaction appeared complete. There was a signed sales agreement, an invoice, and shipping documents showing that the goods had been transferred to a third-party warehouse. However, the auditor discovered that the affiliate had little operating history, limited working capital, and no established customer base capable of absorbing such a large volume of product. The affiliate had made only a small down payment, with the remaining balance due under unusually extended terms.

As the auditor examined the arrangement further, it became clear that the goods had not truly left Meridian's economic control. Meridian agreed to cover the warehouse fees, guaranteed the affiliate against loss on resale, and committed informally to repurchase any unsold items after six months. Internal emails described the transaction as a way to "clean up the balance sheet before year-end." The affiliate had no practical business reason to acquire the inventory other than to assist the parent-related company. Although the paperwork supported a recorded sale, the arrangement did not meaningfully transfer the risks and rewards of ownership. The transaction lacked economic substance because it created favorable accounting results without a real change in the company's economic position.

Non-arm's-length pricing is another important warning sign. Related parties often have the ability to set prices, terms, and conditions without the market discipline that would exist between unrelated parties. That flexibility can be used innocently for internal group purposes, but it also creates risk that recorded amounts do not reflect fair value or ordinary commercial behavior. A company may sell goods to an affiliate at inflated prices to increase reported revenue, purchase services at above-market rates to move profit to another entity, or transfer assets at values chosen to achieve a desired accounting result rather than to reflect actual worth. Auditors should compare related-party pricing to observable market data, prior transactions with independent parties, cost structures, and the economic roles of the parties involved. When pricing differs significantly from normal practice and management cannot explain the reason persuasively, the transaction deserves deeper scrutiny. Non-arm's-length pricing may affect revenue, expenses, asset valuations, tax positions, and disclosures, making it one of the most consequential related-party red flags.

Round-trip transactions are another classic area of concern. These occur when funds, goods, or obligations move between related parties in a circular manner that creates the appearance of business activity without changing the group's underlying economic position. For example, one entity may sell goods to an affiliate while simultaneously agreeing to repurchase them, or cash may be transferred through multiple related entities and then returned in a way that temporarily inflates liquidity, revenue, or investment balances. These arrangements may be complex in form but hollow in substance. Their purpose is often to create an accounting effect, not to carry out a legitimate transaction. Auditors should be alert to offsetting transactions, closely timed reciprocal entries, contracts that mirror one another, or patterns in which recorded sales and purchases among affiliates reverse soon after period-end. Round-trip activity is especially risky because it can make reported revenue, cash flow, or asset activity appear more robust than it truly is. When related-party transactions form a loop rather than a genuine exchange, the accounting presentation may be materially misleading.

EXAMPLE

A real telecommunications example is Qwest Communications' IRU[1] capacity swaps. The SEC alleged that when ordinary demand for fiber capacity weakened, Qwest entered into reciprocal swaps in which it bought IRUs from other telecom companies in exchange for agreements from those same companies to buy IRUs from Qwest. The SEC said these swaps were used to "fill the gap" between actual performance and management's revenue targets.

The core problem was that the transactions created revenue without a meaningful change in economic position. According to the SEC, Qwest recognized upfront revenue on swap transactions even though the assets exchanged were similar fiber-optic capacity, which meant that revenue should not have been recognized the way Qwest reported it. The SEC also alleged that Qwest failed to disclose the swaps properly as nonmonetary transactions.

In practical terms, this is a classic round-trip pattern. Qwest was not simply making an independent sale to an outside customer with genuine demand. Instead, the company was entering into offsetting telecom-capacity deals with counterparties that were also selling similar capacity back to Qwest. The SEC further alleged that Qwest used side agreements and other devices

---

[1] An IRU, or indefeasible right of use, is a long-term contractual right to use a specified amount of telecommunications network capacity, usually on a fiber-optic cable, for a stated period.

to support the desired accounting result. For an auditor, that combination of reciprocal structure, similar assets, and revenue pressure is exactly why telecom capacity swaps became a textbook red flag.

Loans to executives or affiliates also deserve close attention. Such loans may be legal and properly approved in some settings, but they create heightened risk because they blur the line between business transactions and private financial arrangements. A loan to an executive, owner, or affiliated entity may not be collectible on ordinary terms, may lack formal documentation, or may be used to move value out of the company without transparent disclosure. Warning signs include loans with no repayment schedule, repeated renewals, below-market interest rates, repayments funded indirectly by the company itself, or balances that remain outstanding for long periods without enforcement. Auditors should consider whether the loan has economic substance, whether collectability is realistic, and whether the terms resemble those that would be granted to an unrelated borrower. These arrangements can affect classification, valuation, disclosure, and even the integrity of governance, particularly when approval processes are weak or dominated by interested parties.

Complex ownership relationships are another major source of risk in related-party auditing. When ownership is layered across holding companies, family trusts, shell entities, joint ventures, or cross-investments, it may become difficult to determine who actually controls a transaction or benefits from it. Complexity can obscure influence that would otherwise be obvious, making it easier for management to claim that a party is independent when meaningful connections exist. Auditors should examine organizational charts, shareholder records, board composition, financing arrangements, and legal documents to understand where control and influence truly reside. The issue is not merely whether ownership is complicated, but whether the complexity reduces transparency or appears designed to conceal affiliations. In some cases, the related-party relationship is not hidden outright, but it is buried within a structure that makes it difficult to evaluate the real economics of transactions. Where ownership relationships are hard to untangle, the risk of incomplete disclosure and misleading accounting increases substantially.

EXAMPLE

During the audit of Silver Gate Holdings, the auditor was told that a major supplier, North Coast Materials, was an independent third party selected through ordinary purchasing procedures. On the surface, the ownership records appeared to support that claim. North Coast was owned by a limited liability company, which in turn was held by two family trusts and a private investment vehicle. However, when the auditor reviewed the trust documents, board minutes, and loan agreements, a more complicated picture emerged. One family trust benefited the chief executive officer's adult children, while the investment vehicle had been financed with guarantees from Silver Gate's founder. In addition, one of North Coast's directors also served on the board of an affiliate of Silver Gate. None of these links had been identified in the company's related-party disclosure process.

The concern was not simply that the ownership chain was complicated, but that the complexity made the relationship difficult to detect and easy to minimize. Silver Gate had routed a large volume of purchases through North Coast at prices above those charged by other vendors, yet management insisted that the arrangement was entirely independent. Further review showed that contract terms were negotiated outside the normal bidding process and approved by a small group of executives. Because the real pattern of influence was buried within layered entities, trusts, and guarantees, the company was able to present the supplier as unrelated when meaningful connections clearly existed.

Related-party transaction red flags often appear together. An undisclosed affiliate may engage in a transaction lacking substance, at a non-arm's-length price, financed through a loan, within a complex ownership structure. A round-trip transaction may be disguised as ordinary sales activity. A loan may support the affiliate's purchase of the company's own products. For that reason, auditors should evaluate related-party issues as patterns rather than isolated technical matters. The central question is whether the transaction reflects genuine business activity between parties acting with independent interests, or whether the relationship has shaped the accounting outcome in a way that users of the financial statements would not expect.

A careful review of related-party red flags helps the auditor assess disclosure, substance, valuation, and presentation in one of the most manipulation-prone areas of financial reporting. Undisclosed relationships, economically hollow transactions, unusual pricing, circular arrangements, insider loans, and opaque ownership structures all suggest that the financial statements may not fully portray what is really happening. When these warning signs appear, the auditor should respond with greater skepticism, stronger corroboration, and a deliberate focus on substance over form.

Going Concern Red Flags

The going concern assumption is a fundamental basis of financial reporting. It assumes that an entity will continue operating for the foreseeable future and will be able to realize its assets and settle its obligations in the normal course of business rather than through forced liquidation or severe financial distress. For auditors, going concern red flags are especially important because they can affect asset valuation, liability classification, disclosure adequacy, and the overall reliability of the financial statements. A company may continue issuing financial statements on a going concern basis even while serious warning signs suggest that its ability to remain in operation is deteriorating. The auditor's role is not to predict the future with certainty, but to evaluate whether conditions and events raise substantial doubt about the entity's ability to continue as a going concern and whether management's assessment and disclosures are appropriate. This requires careful attention to patterns of financial weakness, operational dependence, legal exposure, and liquidity pressure that may indicate a deeper threat to the company's viability.

One of the most common going concern red flags is recurring operating losses. A single loss period does not necessarily indicate a going concern problem, since losses may arise from temporary events, seasonal patterns, restructuring efforts, or short-term market disruptions. However, repeated losses over multiple periods suggest that the company's core operations may not be generating sustainable earnings. Recurring losses can erode working capital, reduce retained earnings, weaken lender confidence, and limit the company's ability to invest in operations or absorb unexpected setbacks. Auditors should look beyond the net loss figure itself and consider whether the business model appears capable of returning to profitability in a realistic time frame. Management may explain losses as temporary, but those explanations should be evaluated against actual operating trends, margins, fixed cost structure, and industry conditions. If the company repeatedly loses money from ordinary operations, the risk increases that its resources will eventually be exhausted or that management will resort to increasingly aggressive accounting or financing strategies to delay financial deterioration from becoming more visible.

Negative cash flows from operations are another major warning sign, and in many cases they are even more revealing than operating losses. A company can sometimes report accounting income while still suffering cash strain if receivables are not collected, inventory builds excessively, liabilities are paid more quickly, or earnings are supported by noncash items. Persistent negative operating cash flows indicate that the business is not generating enough cash from its core activities to support itself. This condition may force the company to rely on external financing, delay payments, liquidate assets, or seek concessions from creditors and suppliers. For auditors, the pattern and causes of negative operating cash flows are critical. A one-time working capital swing may not be alarming, but repeated negative cash flow from operations often suggests deeper problems in pricing, collections, demand, cost control, or business viability. Auditors should consider whether management's plans to improve cash generation are specific, achievable, and supported by evidence. A business that repeatedly consumes cash through operations is at greater risk of not being able to continue unless it has reliable access to other funding sources.

EXAMPLE

At year-end, Summit Office Products reported a small net profit, but its statement of cash flows showed a third consecutive year of negative cash flow from operations. The primary causes were growing accounts receivable, rising inventory levels, and shrinking trade payables. Management had expanded sales by offering extended payment terms to customers, but collections slowed significantly and many invoices remained unpaid well past due dates. At the same time, the company continued producing inventory in anticipation of demand that did not materialize, causing cash to be tied up in unsold goods. Suppliers had also begun tightening credit terms, so the company was paying cash more quickly than in prior years. Although earnings appeared positive, the underlying business was consuming cash rather than generating it.

The auditor viewed this pattern as a major warning sign because the company's apparent profitability was not translating into liquidity. Management claimed that cash flow would improve soon, but its plan depended on optimistic sales growth and faster collections without persuasive support. A review of post-year-end activity showed continued slow collections, additional borrowing under the line of credit, and discussions with key vendors about delayed payments. The company had avoided reporting large losses partly because of noncash accounting items and aggressive working capital assumptions, but those measures did not solve the cash problem.

The repeated negative operating cash flows suggested deeper weakness in the business model and raised substantial doubt about the company's ability to sustain operations without continued outside financing.

Debt covenant violations are another important going concern red flag because they can trigger immediate financial consequences. Covenants often require a company to maintain specified levels of liquidity, net worth, leverage ratios, interest coverage, or profitability. If the company violates those terms, the lender may gain the right to demand repayment, accelerate maturities, increase borrowing costs, or impose additional restrictions. Even when lenders do not immediately exercise those rights, covenant violations signal that the business may already be under financial stress. Auditors should review loan agreements carefully and assess whether the company has breached existing covenants or is at significant risk of doing so. It is not enough to rely on management's general statement that the bank has been supportive. The auditor should evaluate whether formal waivers have been obtained, whether they were received on a timely basis, and whether the company is likely to remain in compliance going forward. Covenant problems can quickly transform a manageable liquidity issue into a going concern crisis if financing becomes callable or access to additional borrowing is cut off.

Dependence on short-term financing is another warning sign that deserves careful attention. A company that funds long-term assets or recurring operating needs with short-term borrowings may face serious refinancing risk, especially if lenders become less willing to extend credit or if market conditions tighten. Short-term debt can create a recurring cycle of rollover pressure in which the company must continually renegotiate financing simply to remain operational. This is particularly dangerous when the business already has weak cash flow, limited collateral, or deteriorating financial ratios. Auditors should consider not only the amount of short-term financing, but also the nature of the dependence. If the company cannot meet payroll, purchase inventory, or satisfy other ordinary obligations without drawing repeatedly on lines of credit or bridge financing, that dependence may indicate that the core business is not self-sustaining. Management may assume that financing will remain available, but those assumptions should be assessed in light of lender relationships, covenant compliance, market conditions, and the company's recent borrowing history. Heavy reliance on short-term funding often means that even a modest disruption in credit access could threaten continuation of operations.

EXAMPLE

At year-end, Harbor Lane Distributors financed most of its working capital and part of its warehouse expansion through a revolving line of credit and a series of 90-day notes. Although some short-term borrowing was normal in the industry, Harbor Lane had become heavily dependent on these facilities to cover payroll, vendor payments, and routine operating expenses. The company's operating cash flows had been weak for several periods, and it had little unused borrowing capacity remaining. Even so, management continued to treat the debt as a stable funding source and assumed that each maturing obligation would be renewed without difficulty.

The auditor became concerned because this financing structure exposed the company to constant rollover risk. The short-term debt was supporting not only seasonal inventory needs, but also longer-term assets and recurring cash deficits. In addition, the company had come close to violating a debt covenant tied to its current ratio, and recent correspondence with the lender showed increasing scrutiny of borrowing requests. When the auditor reviewed post-year-end activity, the company had already requested a temporary waiver and was negotiating extensions under tighter terms, including higher interest rates and additional collateral. Management's forecast assumed continued lender support, but there was little objective evidence to show that credit would remain available on acceptable terms. The heavy reliance on short-term financing suggested that even a small interruption in borrowing capacity could prevent the company from meeting ordinary obligations and could quickly place continued operations at risk.

The loss of major customers or suppliers is another significant going concern red flag because it can undermine the company's operating base quickly. A business that depends heavily on one or a few customers may experience severe revenue decline if a key relationship ends, contracts are not renewed, or customers shift to competitors. Likewise, heavy reliance on a small number of suppliers can create operational disruption, cost increases, or production delays if those suppliers fail, terminate the relationship, or change terms unfavorably. Auditors should assess customer and supplier concentration, recent contract developments, and whether the company has realistic alternatives if a major relationship is lost. The risk is especially acute when the customer or supplier represents a critical share of sales volume, raw materials, distribution, or specialized services that cannot easily be replaced. Management may express confidence in replacing lost business, but the auditor should consider whether that expectation is supported by concrete plans, market conditions, and past performance. Significant concentration risk can create going concern issues even when the financial statements still appear stable, because the economic dependence may not be fully visible in current-period results.

Pending litigation or regulatory actions also deserve close scrutiny in a going concern assessment. Legal and regulatory matters can create uncertainty not only through potential monetary loss, but also through business disruption, reputational damage, licensing consequences, and restrictions on future operations. A major lawsuit, government investigation, environmental claim, tax dispute, or compliance failure can threaten liquidity and viability if the possible outcomes are severe enough. Even before a final resolution is reached, such matters may affect financing relationships, customer confidence, supplier terms, and management's ability to operate normally. Auditors should evaluate the nature of the claims, the likely range of outcomes, the adequacy of recorded accruals and disclosures, and whether the matter could impair the entity's ability to continue operating. Management may minimize the risk, particularly when litigation is ongoing, but the auditor must assess whether the entity could withstand an adverse result or the costs of prolonged uncertainty. In some cases, the issue is not only the ultimate financial penalty, but the broader operational consequences of regulatory restrictions or damaged market credibility.

EXAMPLE

At year-end, Green Horizon Waste Services was facing a state environmental enforcement action related to alleged contamination at one of its disposal sites. The company had already incurred significant legal and consulting fees, and regulators were considering penalties, mandatory cleanup measures, and possible restrictions on the site's future operations. Management disclosed the matter briefly in the notes but recorded only a modest accrual, arguing that the ultimate outcome could not yet be determined. At the same time, the site in question represented a substantial share of the company's operating cash flow, and several lenders had begun asking for updated information about the case. Although the company remained in operation, the unresolved action created uncertainty far beyond the possibility of a single fine.

The auditor viewed the matter as a going concern issue because the company's ability to continue depended heavily on retaining access to the site and avoiding a liquidity crisis. If regulators imposed operating restrictions or required immediate remediation spending, the company might not have enough cash or borrowing capacity to absorb the impact. In addition, several customers had begun asking whether service disruptions were likely, and one supplier tightened payment terms because of the uncertainty. Management maintained that it expected a favorable resolution, but had little objective evidence to support that view. The combination of potential monetary loss, operational disruption, and reputational damage suggested that the pending regulatory action could materially threaten the company's ability to continue operating.

Going concern red flags rarely appear in isolation. Recurring losses may coincide with negative operating cash flow. Covenant violations may result from the same pressures that drive dependence on short-term financing. The loss of a major customer may trigger further losses, weaker liquidity, and lender concern. Litigation may worsen financial stress already caused by operational weakness. For that reason, auditors should evaluate going concern issues as an interconnected set of conditions rather than a checklist of independent symptoms. The significance of each red flag often depends on the presence of others and on management's realistic ability to mitigate the combined effects.

A careful review of going concern red flags helps the auditor assess whether the financial statements adequately reflect the company's ability to remain in operation and whether management's disclosures are complete and balanced. Recurring losses, negative cash flow, covenant problems, financing dependence, customer or supplier concentration, and legal or regulatory threats all suggest that the business may face more than routine financial pressure. When these conditions exist, the auditor should respond with heightened skepticism, close evaluation of management's plans, and careful attention to whether substantial doubt has been raised and properly disclosed.

Information Technology Red Flags

Information technology plays a central role in modern financial reporting. Transactions are initiated, processed, summarized, stored, and reported through interconnected systems that often operate with minimal manual intervention. As a result, weaknesses in IT controls can affect large volumes of data across multiple accounts and reporting periods. For auditors, information technology and data red flags are especially important because they may indicate that financial information is incomplete, inaccurate, unauthorized, or vulnerable to manipulation. A company may appear to have orderly accounting records while the underlying systems contain control weaknesses that undermine the reliability of those records. These weaknesses can affect transaction processing, journal entry control, the segregation of duties, master file integrity, interface accuracy, and the preservation of evidence. Auditors therefore need to assess not only what the accounting system reports, but also whether the technological environment supporting that reporting is controlled, secure, and transparent.

One major red flag is inadequate access controls. Access controls determine who can view, enter, edit, approve, or delete information within financial and operational systems. When access is poorly designed or loosely administered, employees may gain the ability to perform incompatible functions, alter sensitive data, or bypass normal review processes. For example, a user who can create vendors, enter invoices, and release payments poses a clear fraud risk. Similarly, a person who can modify customer records and post cash receipts may be able to conceal misappropriation or distort receivable balances. Auditors should assess whether user access is based on job responsibilities, whether access changes are approved and documented, and whether terminated or transferred employees are removed promptly from the system. Inadequate access controls increase the risk that errors and fraud can occur without a visible paper trail, especially in highly automated environments where users rely heavily on the integrity of system-generated reports.

A related warning sign is excessive privileged-user access. Privileged users, such as system administrators, database administrators, and certain IT support personnel, often have elevated rights that allow them to change configurations, grant permissions, alter data, or disable controls. These rights may be necessary for legitimate administrative purposes, but they also present significant risk if not properly restricted and monitored. Excessive privileged access exists when too many individuals hold such authority, when business users are granted administrator-level rights, or when privileged actions are not logged and independently reviewed. The concern is not only that a privileged user could commit fraud directly, but also that such a person could alter records, erase evidence, or facilitate improper actions by others. Auditors should pay close attention when administrative rights are concentrated in one individual, when shared administrator accounts are used, or when management cannot clearly explain how privileged activities are monitored. Elevated access without oversight is a classic condition that weakens the entire control structure.

Weak change-management controls are another important red flag because system changes can directly affect the processing of financial information. Change management refers to the process for developing, testing, approving, and implementing modifications to applications, interfaces, configurations, reports, and underlying system logic. If change controls are weak, an entity may introduce errors into production systems, alter calculations unintentionally, or even make deliberate changes that affect financial results without proper authorization. Examples include modifying revenue recognition rules, changing depreciation calculations, altering interface mappings, or adjusting the report logic used in management review controls. Auditors should evaluate whether system changes are requested formally, tested before implementation, approved by appropriate personnel, and moved into production by someone independent of the developer when feasible. Emergency changes deserve particular scrutiny, since they may bypass ordinary review processes. Weak change-management controls increase the risk that the financial system will not process transactions consistently and that key reports relied upon in the audit may not be trustworthy.

EXAMPLE

During the audit of Apex Industrial Supply, the auditor learned that the company had upgraded its enterprise system during the fourth quarter and made several changes to the order-to-cash module shortly before year-end. One change revised the system logic used to determine when revenue would be recognized on customer shipments. Another modified the mapping between the fixed asset subledger and the general ledger, affecting depreciation expense. Although these changes had a direct impact on financial reporting, the company could not provide complete documentation showing that the modifications had been formally requested, tested, approved, and migrated into production through a controlled process. In several cases, the same information technology employee who made the changes also moved them into the live environment. Management explained that the changes were necessary to meet reporting deadlines, but the evidence of review was limited and inconsistent.

The auditor became concerned when exception reports showed unusual revenue transactions and depreciation amounts that differed from prior patterns. Further inquiry revealed that one system change had caused certain customer orders to be flagged as complete before the required shipping terms had been satisfied, thereby accelerating revenue recognition. Another change altered useful life parameters for a group of equipment, reducing current-period depreciation expense. Because emergency changes had been made without adequate testing or independent approval, the company had introduced errors directly into the financial reporting process. Weak change-management controls meant that the system could not be relied upon fully, and the auditor had to consider whether other unauthorized or poorly tested changes might also have affected reported results.

Missing audit trails are another major IT and data red flag. An audit trail is the record of who initiated, changed, approved, or deleted transactions and master data, along with the timing and nature of those actions. Without an adequate audit trail, it becomes difficult or impossible to reconstruct events, investigate anomalies, or determine accountability for unusual activity. In a financial reporting context, missing or incomplete logs can conceal unauthorized journal entries, master file changes, price adjustments, vendor modifications, or overrides of automated controls. Auditors should be cautious when systems do not retain sufficient logs, when logs can be altered by the same users whose activity they record, or when log retention periods are too short to support the audit. The presence of a sophisticated system is not enough if the system does not preserve evidence of what occurred within it. A missing audit trail weakens both preventive and detective controls because it reduces visibility into how information was changed and by whom.

Unusual system overrides also deserve close attention. Many systems include automated validations, approval workflows, tolerance checks, and edit controls designed to prevent improper entries or flag exceptions. Overrides may be necessary in limited cases, but frequent or poorly controlled overrides suggest that users are bypassing safeguards that were intended to protect data integrity. For example, a company may override credit limits to ship more product, bypass three-way matching to process vendor payments, override inventory warnings to force transactions through the system, or manually release orders that failed an automated review. Auditors should consider not only the number of overrides, but also who performs them, whether they are documented, and whether patterns emerge near period-end or in high-risk transaction areas. An override that repeatedly benefits reported results or circumvents a control without clear justification is particularly concerning. When automated controls are routinely bypassed, the organization may be relying on the appearance of system discipline without actually enforcing it.

EXAMPLE

During the audit of Crestmark Wholesale, the auditor reviewed system logs and noticed a sharp increase in manual overrides during the final two weeks of the fiscal year. Many of the overrides involved releasing customer orders that had been blocked automatically by the system's credit-limit controls. Under normal procedures, customers exceeding approved limits were supposed to remain on hold until credit staff completed a review. Instead, several large orders were manually released by senior sales personnel and a finance manager, often with no explanation beyond "urgent shipment" or "approved by management." The same period also included multiple overrides of three-way match controls in accounts payable, allowing vendor invoices to be processed without matching receiving reports.

The pattern was concerning because the overrides affected both revenue recognition and disbursement controls. By forcing shipments through for customers with weak payment histories, management increased period-end sales while also increasing the risk that receivables would not be collected. On the payables side, bypassing invoice matching created the risk that unsupported or duplicate vendor charges could be recorded and paid. The auditor found that override activity was concentrated near period-end and often benefited reported results by increasing shipments or avoiding operational delays that would have reduced earnings. Documentation was inconsistent, and some overrides were performed by individuals who should not have had that level of access. The frequency and timing of the overrides suggested that automated controls existed in form, but were not being enforced in substance.

Data inconsistencies across systems are another important red flag because modern organizations often rely on multiple applications that exchange information through interfaces, uploads, and reconciliations. Sales systems may feed billing systems, billing systems may feed the general ledger, payroll systems may feed labor costing modules, and inventory systems may feed cost accounting. If data is inconsistent across those systems, it may indicate interface failures, mapping errors, timing gaps, unauthorized adjustments, or poor reconciliation procedures. Examples include customer balances that do not agree between subledgers and the general ledger, inventory quantities that differ across warehouse and accounting systems, or payroll data that does not reconcile to human resources records. Auditors should be alert when management relies on spreadsheets to bridge unexplained differences or when reconciliation items remain unresolved over long periods. Inconsistencies across systems raise the possibility that key reports are incomplete or inaccurate, especially when management cannot explain which system should be regarded as authoritative. In a highly automated environment, reliable data flow is essential to reliable financial reporting.

Cybersecurity incidents affecting financial reporting represent another critical red flag. A cyber event may involve unauthorized access, ransomware, data deletion, system outages, phishing attacks, or exfiltration of sensitive information. Even when an incident appears operational rather than accounting-related, it can still affect financial reporting by disrupting transaction processing, impairing system availability, altering data, or exposing control weaknesses. For example, if a ransomware attack disrupts access to accounting records near period-end, management may rely on incomplete data or manual workarounds that increase the risk of misstatement. If attackers gain access to financial systems, they may alter vendor banking information, manipulate payment instructions, or compromise the integrity of reports used for closing and audit purposes. Auditors should evaluate the timing, scope, and remediation of cybersecurity incidents, as well as whether management has assessed the potential effect on financial reporting controls and disclosures. A cyber incident is not just an IT issue. It may have direct implications for the completeness, accuracy, and reliability of the financial statements.

EXAMPLE

During the audit of Meridian Health Products, the auditor learned that the company had experienced a ransomware attack three days before year-end. The attack disrupted access to the enterprise resource planning system, locked key accounting files, and prevented the normal processing of accounts payable, inventory movements, and cash receipts. In response, management shifted to manual spreadsheets and email-based approvals so that it could complete the close on time. Although operations resumed partially after several days, the company could not demonstrate that all transactions recorded during the outage were complete or that the restored data matched the original records. In addition, several vendor banking changes had been processed shortly before the attack, raising concern that unauthorized payment information might have been inserted into the system.

The auditor viewed the incident as a significant financial reporting risk because it affected both system integrity and control performance during a critical reporting period. Reconciliations were delayed, exception reports were unavailable, and several automated controls over payment processing and journal entry review had been bypassed. Further investigation showed that some receiving transactions had not been uploaded properly after the system came back online, which created differences between inventory records and the general ledger. Management initially described the cyberattack as an operational inconvenience, but the event had direct implications for the reliability of the financial statements. The need to rely on manual workarounds, incomplete records, and potentially compromised master data created a heightened risk of material misstatement.

These information technology and data red flags often interact. Weak access controls may coexist with excessive privileged access. Poor change management may lead to data inconsistencies across systems. Missing audit trails may conceal unusual overrides. A cyber incident may expose broader weaknesses in user administration and monitoring. For that reason, auditors should evaluate IT red flags as part of an integrated control environment rather than as isolated technical issues. A system can appear efficient while still being vulnerable to unauthorized change, incomplete processing, and unreliable reporting.

A careful review of information technology and data red flags helps the auditor assess whether the systems supporting financial reporting can be relied upon. Inadequate access restrictions, excessive administrator rights, weak system change discipline, incomplete audit trails, frequent overrides, inconsistent data, and cyber-related disruption all suggest that the accounting information produced by the organization may require greater skepticism and additional testing. In a modern audit, reliable financial reporting depends heavily on reliable systems. When the technological environment is weak, the auditor must assume that risks may extend beyond one application or one account and may affect the integrity of the reporting process as a whole.

Analytical Procedure Red Flags

Analytical procedures are one of the most valuable tools available to auditors because they help reveal patterns, inconsistencies, and relationships that may not be obvious from detailed transaction testing alone. By comparing financial and nonfinancial information across periods, against expectations, and against industry benchmarks, auditors can identify unusual results that warrant further investigation. Analytical procedures do not by themselves prove that a misstatement exists, but they often provide some of the earliest warning signs that financial reporting may not align with the underlying economics of the business. For that reason, red flags identified through analytical procedures are especially important in both audit planning and substantive review. They can direct the auditor toward accounts, locations, products, or transactions where the risk of error or fraud may be elevated. A strong analytical review does more than highlight differences. It asks whether the reported numbers make sense in light of the company's operations, environment, and known business conditions.

One common red flag is an unexpected fluctuation in key financial ratios. Ratios such as current ratio, receivables turnover, inventory turnover, gross margin percentage, debt-to-equity ratio, return on assets, and days sales outstanding often provide insight into changes in the company's financial condition and operating performance. When these ratios change sharply without a clear explanation, the auditor should consider whether the shift reflects a real business development or a possible misstatement. For example, a sudden improvement in receivables turnover might seem positive, but it could also reflect aggressive write-offs, timing differences, or the reclassification of balances. A deterioration in inventory turnover may suggest valuation issues or weakening demand. Ratios are especially useful because they convert raw numbers into relationships that can expose problems hidden within account balances. An unusual ratio change does not automatically indicate an error, but it should prompt the auditor to understand what caused the change and whether that cause is supported by evidence.

Another important analytical red flag is a trend that appears inconsistent with broader industry conditions. A company does not operate in isolation, and its reported results should generally be understandable in the context of what is happening in its market. If competitors are facing declining demand, margin pressure, supply chain disruption, or rising financing costs, yet the audited company reports unusually strong growth and stable profitability without a compelling explanation, the auditor should investigate further. This does not mean that outperformance is impossible. A company may genuinely benefit from better execution, a differentiated product, or market share gains. However, when reported trends diverge materially from industry realities, there is a risk that accounting assumptions, cutoff decisions, or classification choices are masking underlying problems. Auditors should compare company results to external data, peer performance, and known economic conditions. A business that appears immune to adverse market trends may indeed be exceptional, but it may also be misstated.

EXAMPLE

During the audit of Falcon Home Furnishings, the auditor noted that the company reported a 14 percent increase in sales and stable gross margins for the year, even though most competitors in the furniture industry were reporting weaker demand, heavy discounting, and higher freight and financing costs. Trade publications, analyst commentary, and peer financial statements all pointed to slowing consumer purchases and rising pressure on profitability. Management explained Falcon's results by claiming superior sales execution and stronger customer loyalty, but it provided little objective evidence that would justify such a sharp divergence from the rest of the market. There had been no major product launch, no significant store expansion, and no obvious shift in strategy that would explain the outperformance.

The auditor became concerned because the company's results did not align with broader industry conditions or with its own operating indicators. Inventory levels were rising, customer returns increased after year-end, and accounts receivable had grown faster than sales. Further testing showed that a number of large shipments had been recorded as year-end sales even though some goods remained in transit or were subject to unusual return rights. In addition, certain freight and promotional costs had been classified below gross profit rather than in the cost of sales, which helped preserve margins. The issue was not simply that Falcon had a good year. Rather, its reported growth and profitability appeared inconsistent with market reality, and further audit work suggested that aggressive revenue cutoff and expense classification decisions were masking weaker underlying performance.

Margin anomalies are another significant warning sign. Gross margin, operating margin, and net margin patterns often reveal whether reported costs and revenues are moving together in a sensible way. If margins improve sharply without corresponding operational changes, if one product line consistently produces improbable returns, or if margins remain stable despite volatile input costs or pricing pressure, the auditor should consider whether the relationship between revenue and expense has been distorted. Margin anomalies can arise from improper capitalization, understated cost of sales, inaccurate inventory valuation, premature revenue recognition, or the use of reserves to smooth results. They can also reflect classification issues, such as moving ordinary operating expenses below the operating income line. Auditors should analyze margins by product, customer, geography, and time period when possible, because anomalies often become more visible at a disaggregated level than in the aggregate financial statements. A margin that appears unusually favorable may be the result of genuine efficiency, but it may also signal that one side of the earnings equation is not being recorded appropriately.

EXAMPLE

During the audit of Summit Precision Tools, the auditor observed that gross margin had risen from 28 percent to 36 percent in the fourth quarter, even though raw material prices had increased and competitors were reporting margin compression. Management attributed the improvement to better production efficiency, but plant reports showed no major process changes, labor productivity gains, or purchasing advantages that would explain such a large increase. A closer analysis by product line revealed that the margin improvement was concentrated in one group of industrial parts that had historically generated average, not exceptional, profitability. The anomaly was even more pronounced in the final month of the year.

The auditor expanded her testing and found several accounting issues that distorted the relationship between revenue and cost. First, a portion of routine factory overhead and equipment repair costs had been capitalized into fixed assets rather than being included in current manufacturing expense. Second, inventory records for the high-margin product line contained standard costs that had not been updated to reflect recent increases in material inputs, which caused the cost of sales to be understated when items were sold. Third, certain quarter-end shipments had been recorded as revenue before all shipping terms were satisfied, increasing sales without a corresponding proper recognition of related costs. When these items were analyzed together, the margin improvement no longer appeared to reflect operational strength. Instead, it suggested that the company's reported profitability had been inflated by a mix of improper capitalization, understated cost of sales, and aggressive revenue recognition practices.

Unusual relationships among accounts are another important category of analytical red flags. Financial statement accounts are linked economically, and when those relationships stop behaving in expected ways, the auditor should understand why. For example, if revenue increases substantially while accounts receivable grow even faster and cash collections lag, the relationship may suggest aggressive credit practices or premature revenue recognition. If inventory rises while cost of sales remains flat and turnover declines, the issue may involve slow-moving goods, production inefficiencies, or inflated inventory values. If prepaid expenses expand without a similar pattern in the underlying expenditures, there may be classification problems. Likewise, if accrued liabilities decline while payroll or other operating activity remains stable, the company may be understating its obligations. These inter-account relationships are useful because they test whether the financial statements tell a coherent story. When balances move in ways that do not align with one another, it often means that one or more accounts are incomplete, misstated, or affected by unusual transactions. Auditors should not evaluate account balances in isolation when the broader relationship among them suggests inconsistency.

Budget-to-actual variances also provide valuable red flag information. Management budgets are not always accurate, and variances from the budget are not automatically suspicious. However, large or repeated variances can indicate areas where assumptions were unrealistic, controls are weak, or actual results are being influenced by unusual accounting. A significant favorable variance may warrant just as much attention as an unfavorable one. For example, if revenue exceeds budget by a large amount near period-end, the auditor should consider whether sales were accelerated, terms were loosened, or returns are likely to increase later. If expenses come in well below budget without an operational explanation, management may have deferred costs, capitalized expenses, or reduced accruals. Budget-to-actual analysis is especially useful when management closely monitors budget performance for compensation or debt covenant purposes, since those incentives may increase the risk of result-driven accounting decisions. Auditors should review not only the size of variances, but also management's explanations and whether those explanations are supported by actual business conditions.

Nonfinancial data that is inconsistent with reported financial results is one of the most powerful analytical red flags available to auditors. Financial reporting should generally align with operational measures such as units sold, production volume, headcount, store traffic, occupancy rates, shipment counts, project milestones, or customer retention levels. When reported revenue, margins, or asset balances do not make sense in relation to these nonfinancial indicators, the inconsistency may reveal that the accounting does not reflect operational reality. For example, a manufacturing company may report strong sales growth even though production volume and shipping data are flat. A retailer may report higher revenue despite declining transaction counts and store traffic. A service company may show rising revenue without a corresponding increase in billable hours, contracts completed, or staffing capacity. These mismatches matter because nonfinancial data is often harder to manipulate in the same way as accounting estimates and classifications. Auditors should therefore use operational information as a reasonableness check on the financial statements. When the company's nonfinancial activity does not support the reported results, there is a strong basis for deeper inquiry.

EXAMPLE

During the audit of Valley Crest Packaging, the auditor noted that reported revenue had increased by 18 percent over the prior year, and management highlighted the growth as evidence of strong customer demand. However, several nonfinancial indicators did not support that result. Production reports showed that unit output had remained essentially flat, shipping records reflected only a minor increase in outbound deliveries, and warehouse activity logs showed no meaningful rise in order volume. In addition, the company had not added production shifts, expanded capacity, or hired additional plant staff that would normally be expected if sales had truly grown at that rate. The reported financial improvement appeared disconnected from the company's actual operating activity.

Because of this mismatch, the auditor performed deeper testing of year-end transactions. The review showed that a number of sales had been recorded before goods were shipped, while other transactions involved bill-and-hold arrangements that lacked persuasive support for revenue recognition. Some orders were also recorded at full value even though side agreements granted customers broad return rights and delayed delivery options. When the auditor compared monthly revenue trends to production volume and shipment counts, the inconsistency was most significant near period-end, when management was under pressure to meet earnings targets. The nonfinancial data provided a strong reasonableness check that the reported growth was not genuine. Rather than reflecting improved business performance, the financial statements appeared to include revenue that had been recognized too early or without sufficient operational support.

Analytical red flags are most effective when they are considered together rather than one at a time. An unexpected ratio change may coincide with margin anomalies. Industry outperformance may be accompanied by weak cash flow and rising receivables. Budget variances may align with unusual account relationships. Nonfinancial inconsistencies may reinforce concerns already raised by trend analysis. When several analytical signals point in the same direction, the risk of material misstatement becomes much more significant. The value of analytical procedures lies not only in identifying isolated oddities, but also in helping the auditor form a broader view of whether the financial statements reflect a plausible and internally consistent picture of the business.

A careful analytical review helps the auditor determine whether reported results are economically credible. Unexpected ratio movements, trends that do not match industry conditions, unusual margin patterns, inconsistent account relationships, large budget variances, and mismatches between operational data and financial reporting all suggest that further investigation may be necessary. These red flags do not replace detailed audit evidence, but they help direct attention to where that evidence is most needed. In many audits, analytical procedures provide the first indication that something in the financial statements does not fit. When that happens, the auditor should treat the inconsistency not as a curiosity to be explained away, but as a signal that the underlying accounting may deserve much closer scrutiny.

Audit Evidence Red Flags

Audit evidence and documentation are central to the auditor's ability to form a conclusion about whether the financial statements are fairly presented. Even when account balances appear reasonable on the surface, the quality, consistency, and reliability of supporting evidence can reveal important warning signs. In many audits, red flags do not first emerge from analytical procedures or technical accounting issues. Instead, they appear in the way records are maintained, how information is produced, and how personnel respond when evidence is requested. Weak or unusual documentation does not automatically mean that fraud or material misstatement exists, but it often indicates that the auditor should apply greater skepticism and expand procedures. Reliable financial reporting depends on the existence of underlying records that are complete, authentic, timely, and consistent with the company's explanations. When those features are missing, the risk attached to the related accounts rises substantially.

One of the most basic but important warning signs is missing documentation. Transactions that affect the financial statements should ordinarily be supported by contracts, invoices, receiving reports, shipping records, reconciliations, approvals, correspondence, or other relevant evidence. When these materials are unavailable, incomplete, or cannot be located for significant transactions, the auditor should question whether the transaction was valid, properly authorized, accurately recorded, or even occurred at all. Missing documents may result from weak filing practices or poor system organization, but they may also indicate an attempt to conceal improper activity. The risk becomes greater when missing documentation relates to unusual transactions, period-end entries, significant estimates, or areas already associated with elevated audit risk. Auditors should consider whether the absence is isolated and understandable or whether it reflects a broader pattern of poor record discipline. A company that cannot produce support for material items weakens the credibility of its financial reporting process, since undocumented accounting is inherently harder to verify and easier to manipulate.

Altered or photocopied records are another significant red flag because they raise immediate questions about authenticity. A photocopy is not inherently suspicious, since many organizations store documents electronically or maintain scanned images rather than original paper records. However, when only copies are available for critical items, when the copies appear incomplete, or when marks, overwriting, inconsistent fonts, or irregular formatting suggest that information may have been changed, the auditor should proceed carefully. Altered records may indicate that a transaction was modified after the fact, that supporting evidence was created to justify an entry already recorded, or that management is attempting to replace missing originals with less reliable substitutes. The issue is not only whether the document exists, but whether it can be trusted as a faithful representation of the original transaction. Auditors should compare questionable documents to other sources of evidence, such as system logs, third-party correspondence, bank records, or independent confirmations. Where authenticity is doubtful, the evidential value of the document falls sharply. A seemingly small inconsistency in a key document can have significant implications if it suggests that the company's records are being curated to support a preferred conclusion rather than to reflect what actually occurred.

Conflicting explanations from personnel are another important source of audit red flags. When different employees describe the same transaction, process, or event in inconsistent ways, the auditor should consider whether there is confusion, weak internal communication, or something more serious. Honest misunderstandings do occur, especially in complex organizations, but repeated contradictions can indicate that the underlying facts are not well controlled or that individuals are attempting to shape the narrative in ways that protect themselves or management. For example, accounting staff may describe a journal entry as routine while operations personnel say the related transaction was unusual. A sales manager may explain a customer arrangement one way, while the legal department describes materially different contract terms. Conflicting explanations become especially significant when they involve sensitive topics such as revenue cutoff, related-party dealings, reserve judgments, or unusual transactions near period-end. Auditors should not accept the first explanation that sounds plausible. They should reconcile the inconsistencies, determine which version aligns with documentary evidence, and assess whether the conflicting responses suggest a deeper reliability problem within the entity. In many cases, inconsistency in personnel explanations is not the issue itself, but a signal that the supporting facts may not be as straightforward as management claims.

EXAMPLE

During the audit of Northfield Medical Devices, the auditor asked several employees about a large year-end sale recorded on the last day of the reporting period. The accounting manager described the entry as a routine shipment to a long-standing customer and said that all revenue recognition criteria had been satisfied before year-end. However, the shipping supervisor stated that the goods were still in the company's staging area on the evening of the last day of the year and were not actually picked up by the carrier until the following morning. When the auditor spoke with the sales manager, he explained that the customer had "committed" to the purchase before year-end and that shipment timing was not important because the order was considered final. The legal department gave yet another explanation, noting that the contract included a side letter allowing the customer to delay delivery and cancel part of the order if market demand weakened.

These conflicting descriptions caused the auditor to expand testing rather than accept management's initial explanation. Documentary review showed that the invoice had been issued before shipment, the bill of lading was dated the next period, and the side letter had not been provided during the initial contract review. The inconsistencies among accounting, operations, sales, and legal personnel suggested that the transaction was not a straightforward routine sale. Instead, the differing stories pointed to a possible attempt to justify premature revenue recognition after the fact. The conflicting explanations were therefore not just a communication problem. They were a warning sign that the recorded transaction may not have occurred in the manner management originally described.

Delays in providing requested information are also important warning signs. In most audits, some delay is normal, especially when requests involve archived materials, multiple departments, or highly detailed schedules. However, repeated or unusual delays can suggest disorganization, weak records management, or possible reluctance to provide evidence that may raise questions. The timing of the delay matters. If requested information is withheld until after the auditor has moved on, or if it is produced only after repeated follow-up and then arrives in an incomplete or changed form, the auditor should consider whether the delay was merely operational or whether it served to manage the audit process. Delays are especially concerning when they relate to high-risk areas, significant estimates, large adjustments, or unusual transactions. A company that is slow to provide evidence may be struggling to find support for what has already been recorded, or it may be attempting to reduce the auditor's ability to investigate effectively within reporting deadlines. Timely access to information is an important part of audit transparency, and when that access is impaired, the auditor should treat the condition as potentially meaningful.

Overreliance on management-produced reports is another common documentation-related red flag. Many audits necessarily use reports generated by the company's systems, including aging reports, inventory listings, exception reports, revenue schedules, reserve calculations, and journal entry extracts. These reports can be useful and often essential, but they are less persuasive when the auditor does not understand how they are generated, whether they are complete and accurate, or whether they can be modified outside controlled processes. The risk becomes greater when management provides summary schedules that are not easily traceable back to source data, or when key audit conclusions depend heavily on internally prepared spreadsheets without independent validation. Auditors should evaluate the reliability of management-produced reports by testing report parameters, reconciling outputs to source systems, reviewing access and change controls, and determining whether the reports are used consistently in the business. A polished report may appear authoritative while still omitting transactions, relying on incorrect filters, or incorporating manual adjustments that are not visible to the auditor. When management-generated information is used without sufficient validation, the audit may rest too heavily on evidence that reflects management's presentation of events rather than independently corroborated facts.

EXAMPLE

During the audit of Crestline Apparel, the auditor relied heavily at first on a management-produced aged receivables report to assess collectability and evaluate the allowance for doubtful accounts. The report showed that most customer balances were current and that overdue amounts had declined at year-end. Management used this schedule to support a relatively low allowance and described it as a standard system-generated report. However, when the auditor asked how the report was produced, accounting personnel gave only a general explanation and could not clearly identify the report parameters, the aging basis, or whether credit memos and unapplied cash were included consistently. The report also existed only as an exported spreadsheet with several hidden columns and manual notes.

Because of these concerns, the auditor performed additional testing. A reconciliation of the report total to the general ledger revealed only a small difference, but a deeper comparison to customer-level source data showed that certain disputed invoices had been excluded through a filter applied after export. In addition, several large past-due balances had been offset manually against pending credits that had not yet been approved. The company's reserve calculation depended directly on this adjusted aging report, so the omissions made the allowance appear lower than it should have been. Further inquiry showed that the spreadsheet had been prepared by one manager without independent review. The issue was not merely that management had prepared the report. It was that the audit evidence appeared reliable on the surface but was not sufficiently validated and therefore reflected management's preferred presentation rather than a complete view of receivable risk.

Inconsistent third-party confirmations represent another serious red flag because external evidence is often among the most persuasive forms of audit support. Confirmations from banks, customers, vendors, lenders, attorneys, warehouse operators, or other outside parties can help validate balances, rights, obligations, and transaction terms. When those confirmations do not agree with the company's records, the auditor must determine why. Some differences are timing-related or administrative, but others may reveal more fundamental problems such as disputed balances, undisclosed side agreements, unrecorded liabilities, nonexistent assets, or altered contract terms. The auditor should not dismiss confirmation differences too quickly, especially when management offers broad explanations without clear corroboration. A customer confirmation that disputes the amount owed, a bank confirmation showing restrictions not recorded by the company, or a legal letter suggesting greater exposure than management disclosed can all point to material risk. External inconsistency is especially important because it challenges the reliability of internally generated evidence. When the company's records and outside evidence do not align, the auditor must resolve the contradiction rather than defaulting to management's version.

EXAMPLE

During the audit of Harbor Industrial Supply, the auditor sent customer confirmations for several large year-end receivable balances. One major customer responded that the amount owed was far lower than the balance shown in Harbor's records and stated that part of the shipment had been returned before year-end. Another customer indicated that it had agreed to purchase the goods only on a consignment basis and did not consider the inventory to be its obligation. Management dismissed these responses as misunderstandings and claimed that the customers' accounting departments were using outdated information. However, management could not immediately provide clear evidence to support its position.

Because the confirmation responses came from external parties, the auditor treated the differences as a significant red flag. Further testing showed that the first customer had, in fact, returned goods that Harbor had not recorded until the next period. In the second case, side correspondence revealed that the customer had broad rights to return unsold items and was not required to pay until resale occurred. Those terms were inconsistent with a completed sale at year-end. The auditor also found internal emails showing pressure to "hold the revenue line" until after the financial statements were issued. The inconsistent confirmations suggested that the company's receivable balances and revenue recognition were not supported by independent third-party evidence. Rather than being minor administrative differences, the confirmation exceptions pointed to disputed sales, unrecorded returns, and terms that undermined the company's accounting treatment.

These red flags from audit evidence and documentation often appear together. Missing records may be accompanied by delays in response. Altered documents may coincide with conflicting explanations from staff. Weak support may force the auditor to rely heavily on management-prepared reports, only to find that third-party evidence tells a different story. For that reason, auditors should not assess documentation issues in isolation. The broader pattern matters. A company that struggles repeatedly to provide consistent, authentic, and timely evidence may present a greater audit risk even if no single issue appears decisive on its own.

A careful evaluation of audit evidence and documentation helps the auditor assess not only the validity of specific transactions, but also the overall reliability of the entity's financial reporting process. Missing documents, questionable records, inconsistent explanations, delays in production, unsupported reliance on internal reports, and contradictions from external confirmations all suggest that the evidence base may be weaker than it first appears. When these warning signs arise, the auditor should respond with heightened skepticism, more persuasive corroboration, and a willingness to question whether the underlying accounting has been supported adequately. In many cases, the quality of the evidence tells the auditor as much about risk as the numbers themselves.

Inquiry Red Flags

Interviews and inquiries are an important part of audit work because they help the auditor understand processes, evaluate the consistency of explanations, identify areas requiring deeper testing, and assess the overall reliability of management's representations. Inquiry alone is not sufficient audit evidence for most significant matters, but it often provides the first indication that something may be wrong. How people respond to questions can reveal much about the quality of internal controls, the transparency of the organization, and the possibility that information is being withheld, distorted, or coordinated. For auditors, inquiry red flags are especially important because they often arise before documentary proof is fully developed. A company may provide complete-looking schedules and reports while the behavior of management and staff suggests that the underlying facts are less stable than the paperwork implies. Evasive answers, inconsistent explanations, resistance to access, hostility, and unusual staffing changes can all indicate that the auditor should increase skepticism and expand procedures.

One common red flag is evasive responses from management. Not every incomplete answer is suspicious, since some questions require follow-up or consultation with others. However, when management consistently avoids direct answers, changes the subject, responds in vague terms, or provides information that sounds plausible without actually addressing the question asked, the auditor should be cautious. Evasion can take many forms. A manager may answer a technical question with a broad statement about company policy, discuss intentions instead of facts, or refer repeatedly to immaterial details while leaving the central issue unresolved. This behavior may indicate weak understanding, but it may also suggest an effort to limit the auditor's ability to identify a problem. Evasive responses are especially concerning in high-risk areas such as revenue recognition, related-party relationships, reserves, legal contingencies, and unusual period-end transactions. Auditors should not treat a polished but indirect response as a satisfactory explanation. The key issue is whether the answer is clear, responsive, and supported by evidence.

EXAMPLE

During the audit of a software company, the auditor asked the controller why a large amount of revenue had been recorded on the last two days of the year. Instead of explaining the specific transactions, the controller responded that the company had a strong culture of meeting customer needs and always followed its revenue policies carefully. When the auditor asked whether the goods had actually been delivered before year-end, the controller shifted to a discussion of how hard the sales team had worked during the quarter. A follow-up question about shipping documents led to another indirect answer, this time about expected customer demand in the coming year.

The auditor then asked for evidence supporting the recorded sales, including contracts, invoices, and proof of delivery. The controller provided a stack of sales reports and highlighted several small routine transactions, but did not address the few large period-end entries that had created most of the revenue increase. When asked again about those entries, the controller said the details were immaterial in the context of annual growth, even though the amounts were individually significant.

This pattern of polished but unresponsive answers raised concern. The issue was not merely poor communication. The controller appeared to be steering attention away from whether the sales met the criteria for revenue recognition, which justified expanded audit testing.

Another warning sign is an overly rehearsed explanation. Some degree of consistency is normal when personnel understand a process well, and management often prepares in advance for audit meetings. Still, explanations become a red flag when they appear scripted, unusually polished, or repeated word-for-word by multiple individuals in a way that suggests coordination rather than genuine understanding. A rehearsed explanation may indicate that management has instructed staff on what to say in order to control the narrative around a sensitive topic. This is particularly concerning when the explanation sounds precise but lacks operational detail, or when staff cannot answer reasonable follow-up questions once the prepared language runs out. The issue is not that management prepared for the audit. The issue is whether the explanation reflects actual knowledge and reality or a coordinated attempt to present a version of events that minimizes scrutiny.

Conflicting statements among employees are another significant inquiry red flag. In a well-controlled organization, people involved in the same process should generally provide compatible explanations, even if they describe different aspects of it. When employees offer materially different accounts of how approvals occur, when transactions were initiated, who authorized a journal entry, or whether a side agreement existed, the inconsistency should not be ignored. Conflicting statements may result from training gaps, weak communication, or decentralized operations, but they may also indicate that the underlying process is poorly controlled or that some individuals are concealing information. The risk becomes greater when the contradictions involve sensitive matters, unusual transactions, or responses that affect key audit assertions. Auditors should compare statements across departments, seniority levels, and functional roles. An inconsistency between management and staff can be especially revealing, since staff may describe the operational reality more candidly than leadership. When interview evidence does not align, the auditor should reconcile the differences through follow-up questions and documentary corroboration rather than selecting the explanation that sounds most convenient.

EXAMPLE

During an audit of inventory, the auditor asked several employees how a large year-end adjustment had been recorded. The warehouse manager said the adjustment was made after a physical count revealed damaged goods that needed to be written down. The controller, however, stated that the entry related to goods in transit that had been temporarily excluded from inventory. When the auditor asked the cost accounting manager, she said the adjustment was intended to correct a pricing error in the standard cost system. These explanations were not minor differences in wording. They pointed to entirely different events, accounting treatments, and supporting evidence.

The inconsistency became more concerning when the auditor asked who had approved the journal entry. The controller said the chief financial officer had reviewed it, while the staff accountant who posted the entry said he had received instructions directly from the controller and was not aware of any higher-level approval. The warehouse supervisor added that no one from accounting had discussed damaged goods with warehouse personnel before year-end.

Because the statements conflicted, the auditor did not accept the most polished explanation. Instead, the auditor obtained the journal entry support, approval records, inventory count sheets, shipping documents, and email correspondence. That follow-up revealed the adjustment had been recorded without adequate support and had the effect of overstating ending inventory, making the conflicting statements an important red flag.

Reluctance to allow auditor access is another important red flag. Auditors need reasonable access to records, systems, locations, and personnel in order to obtain sufficient appropriate evidence. When management restricts access, delays meetings, limits who can be interviewed, insists on being present for routine staff inquiries, or steers the auditor away from certain documents or operational areas, the restriction may indicate more than scheduling difficulty. Access limitations can be a sign that management is attempting to control what the auditor sees and hears. This is particularly concerning when the reluctance involves third-party records, remote locations, significant transactions, or employees likely to have firsthand knowledge of unusual events. Auditors should assess whether the restriction is isolated and justifiable or whether it forms part of a broader pattern of resistance. An open and well-controlled organization may have logistical challenges, but it usually does not resist ordinary audit access without a specific and reasonable explanation. When access becomes an issue, the auditor should consider the implications for scope and the possibility that important evidence is being shielded.

Excessive defensiveness or hostility is another behavioral red flag that can affect the reliability of inquiry responses. Audits can be demanding, and some tension is normal when deadlines are tight or questions are repetitive. However, a strong defensive reaction to ordinary audit questions may suggest that management or staff view the inquiry as threatening because it touches on a weakness, inconsistency, or deliberate misstatement. Hostility may appear as irritation, dismissive language, personal criticism of the audit team, repeated claims that the question is unnecessary, or efforts to portray reasonable follow-up as distrustful or unreasonable. In some cases, management may become defensive when asked about control failures, unusual journal entries, or changes in estimates that improved earnings. Auditors should not interpret every sharp tone as evidence of fraud, but persistent defensiveness in response to standard audit procedures deserves attention. A credible explanation is usually able to withstand scrutiny without emotional resistance. When hostility increases as questions become more specific, it may indicate that the issue is more sensitive than management wants to acknowledge.

Unusual turnover in accounting staff is another valuable inquiry-related red flag because personnel changes can reveal instability in the financial reporting function. Turnover is not automatically suspicious, since people leave for many legitimate reasons. Even so, frequent departures among controllers, chief financial officers, accounting managers, internal auditors, or key operational accounting personnel may indicate stress, poor leadership, disagreement over accounting practices, or broader control problems. This is especially significant when turnover occurs near reporting dates, when replacements are temporary or inexperienced, or when management offers vague or changing explanations for why people left. Auditors should consider whether the turnover has disrupted reconciliations, closing procedures, supervision, or knowledge of significant transactions. They should also assess whether departing personnel were associated with areas currently under audit scrutiny. Sometimes unusual turnover suggests that employees were unwilling to support an accounting position or remain in an environment where controls were being overridden. Even when there is no direct evidence of misconduct, frequent changes in key accounting roles often increase the risk of error and weaken the reliability of management representations.

EXAMPLE

During the audit of a manufacturing company, the auditor learned that the controller had resigned two weeks before year-end, the assistant controller had left three months earlier, and the accounts payable manager was also departing during the fieldwork period. Management explained the changes as routine career moves, but the explanations were vague and differed depending on who was asked. The chief executive officer described the departures as unrelated personal decisions, while the human resources manager mentioned burnout and disagreement over workload. Meanwhile, a temporary consultant had been brought in to help close the books.

The timing of the turnover raised concern because year-end is when the company records reserves, inventory adjustments, and other significant estimates. The auditor found that several account reconciliations were incomplete, closing entries had been posted late, and no one currently on staff could clearly explain a large increase in accrued liabilities recorded at year-end. When asked about the supporting analysis, the temporary consultant said it had been prepared by the former controller, but the file was missing key schedules.

The auditor also learned through inquiry that the departed assistant controller had questioned whether certain production costs should be capitalized into inventory. That information did not prove misconduct, but it suggested possible disagreement over accounting treatment. Because of the unusual turnover, the auditor expanded testing in the affected areas and treated management explanations with greater caution.

These interview and inquiry red flags often reinforce one another. Evasive responses may come from the same individuals who limit access. Rehearsed explanations may coexist with conflicting staff statements. Hostility may intensify when the auditor asks about turnover, unusual transactions, or restricted records. For that reason, auditors should evaluate inquiry-related concerns as patterns of behavior rather than isolated personality traits. The relevance lies not in whether someone seems uncomfortable, but in whether the organization's responses collectively suggest openness, consistency, and control, or instead suggest resistance, coordination, and conccalmcnt.

A careful evaluation of interview and inquiry red flags helps the auditor assess the credibility of management and the reliability of representations that support the financial statements. Evasive answers, scripted explanations, internal contradictions, access resistance, defensive behavior, and unusual staff turnover all suggest that the audit may require stronger corroboration and deeper follow-up. Inquiry is most valuable when it is not treated as a formality. The words people use, the consistency of their explanations, and the way they react to reasonable questions can provide important signals about whether the underlying accounting deserves greater skepticism. In many audits, behavior is not proof, but it is often an early indicator that the documentary evidence may not tell the full story.

Industry-Specific Red Flags

Auditing red flags do not appear in exactly the same form across all entities. While many warning signs are broadly applicable, the business model, regulatory environment, transaction structure, and operating risks of a specific industry often shape where misstatements are most likely to arise. An auditor who understands industry-specific red flags is better positioned to identify unusual patterns that might otherwise seem routine. This matters because management can exploit industry complexity to justify accounting treatments that are aggressive, incomplete, or misleading. In some cases, the same financial statement balance can carry very different risks depending on the type of entity involved. Inventory issues in manufacturing differ from inventory issues in retail. Revenue concerns in construction differ from revenue concerns in software. Therefore, effective red flag analysis requires the auditor to interpret financial results and control conditions in light of the industry's operational realities rather than relying only on generic audit procedures.

In manufacturing, red flags often arise in inventory, production costing, capacity utilization, and overhead allocation. Manufacturers frequently carry large balances of raw materials, work in process, and finished goods, which creates risk around quantity tracking, valuation, and obsolescence. Warning signs include large fluctuations in production variances, persistent negative inventory balances, unexplained adjustments to standard costs, or inventory growth that is not supported by demand trends. Gross margin anomalies may also indicate improper overhead absorption or failure to recognize excess capacity costs appropriately. A plant operating well below normal capacity may still report strong margins if overhead is being capitalized too aggressively into inventory rather than recognized in current-period expense. Other red flags include excessive scrap that is not reflected in cost records, weak controls over the movement of goods between production stages, and delayed recognition of obsolete inventory tied to discontinued product lines. Auditors in manufacturing should connect operational data, such as throughput, machine utilization, yield rates, and work order completion, to the financial statements to determine whether reported costs and asset values are plausible.

EXAMPLE

During the audit of an electronics manufacturer, the auditor noted that finished goods inventory had increased by 28 percent over the prior year even though sales volume had declined. Management explained that the buildup was temporary and related to expected customer demand, yet production reports showed several product lines were operating below normal capacity and some items had not moved in months. At the same time, the company reported stable gross margins, which seemed inconsistent with lower utilization and rising storage costs.

Further inquiry revealed additional warning signs. The cost accountant had made several year-end adjustments to overhead rates, but the supporting analysis was incomplete. Production variance reports showed unusually large favorable overhead variances, while scrap reports from the factory indicated high defect rates that were not reflected in inventory valuation. The auditor also found repeated negative inventory balances in the work-in-process records, suggesting weak tracking of goods between production stages.

When the auditor compared machine utilization, work order completion data, and sales trends to the financial results, the numbers did not align. The plant had substantial idle capacity, yet overhead appeared to be absorbed into inventory as if production were operating at normal levels. In addition, some finished goods related to an older product design were still carried at full standard cost despite minimal demand.

These conditions suggested overstated inventory and understated current-period expense, requiring expanded testing of valuation, obsolescence, and overhead allocations.

In retail and distribution, common red flags center on revenue cutoff, inventory shrinkage, returns, markdowns, and vendor allowances. Retail businesses often process large transaction volumes with relatively thin margins, so even small errors in inventory or pricing can materially affect results. Warning signs include unusual increases in gross margin despite stable or declining sales volume, excessive reliance on markdown reserves that change significantly near period-end, and large post-period returns that cast doubt on year-end sales validity. Inventory issues are also significant because retailers may carry seasonal or fashion-sensitive goods that lose value quickly. Slow-moving stock, weak physical count controls, and unexplained differences between point-of-sale systems and inventory records can all signal valuation or existence problems. In distribution businesses, channel stuffing and end-of-period shipment spikes are especially important, since revenue may be inflated by shipping more product than customers can reasonably absorb. Auditors should also watch for aggressive recognition of vendor rebates, promotional allowances, or cooperative advertising payments, since those items can be used to reduce the cost of sales or operating expenses inappropriately.

EXAMPLE

During the audit of a national apparel retailer, the auditor noted that fourth-quarter gross margin had improved even though same-store sales were flat and heavy holiday promotions had been advertised throughout the season. Management explained the margin increase as the result of better inventory planning, but several red flags suggested otherwise. Year-end inventory included a large volume of winter merchandise that had sold slowly, yet markdown reserves had decreased from the prior year. In addition, a significant number of customer returns were processed in the first two weeks of the new year, many of them tied to sales recorded in the final days of the reporting period.

The auditor also found differences between point-of-sale records and the perpetual inventory system at several store locations. Physical count adjustments were unusually high, suggesting possible shrinkage or weak count procedures. At the distribution center, shipping activity spiked sharply in the last three days of the year, with large orders sent to a few major customers. Subsequent sales reports showed those customers did not sell through the goods quickly, raising the possibility of channel stuffing.

Further review showed that vendor rebates had been recorded as reductions of the cost of sales before the company had met all qualifying purchase or promotional requirements. Taken together, these issues indicated the possible overstatement of revenue, understatement of inventory losses, and improper recognition of vendor allowances.

In construction and long-term contract environments, the most significant red flags often involve revenue recognition, estimated costs to complete, change orders, claims, and job profitability. Because revenue is commonly recognized over time, management's judgments about project stage of completion and total expected cost are central to reported results. A small change in estimated costs can materially change profit recognition. Red flags include projects that remain profitable despite repeated delays, declining gross margins not accompanied by updated forecasts, significant unapproved change orders included in revenue, or claims recognized before recovery is sufficiently supported. Auditors should be especially alert when job schedules are outdated, when project managers provide inconsistent estimates, or when loss contracts are not recognized promptly. Cutoff also matters because costs and billings near period-end may be manipulated to influence reported progress. A project that appears on schedule in the accounting system but is behind operationally may indicate that revenue has been recognized too aggressively. Construction accounting often depends heavily on field-level estimates, so auditors need to compare accounting records to project reports, site conditions, and contract terms rather than relying solely on summary schedules.

EXAMPLE

During the audit of a commercial construction contractor, the auditor reviewed a large office tower project that management continued to report as profitable, even though the job had experienced weather delays, subcontractor disputes, and repeated design revisions. The accounting records showed the project was 72 percent complete and had recognized a substantial portion of the expected profit. However, when the auditor compared that information to internal project reports, the schedule showed the structural phase was behind plan and several major cost categories were trending above budget.

The project manager stated that the margin would recover once pending change orders were approved, but many of those change orders had not yet been signed by the customer. The controller nevertheless included a significant amount of estimated revenue from them in the job profitability report. In addition, a claim for delay damages had been recorded even though supporting correspondence showed the customer was disputing responsibility. When asked about estimated costs to complete, the project manager and estimator gave different answers, and neither could fully explain why the forecast had not been updated despite the delays.

The auditor also noted several supplier invoices dated just after year-end that related to work performed before year-end, suggesting possible cutoff issues. These conditions indicated that revenue may have been recognized too aggressively, forecasts were outdated, and the project might actually be in a loss position requiring immediate recognition.

In software and technology companies, red flags frequently arise in revenue recognition, the capitalization of development costs, contract terms, and the distinction between licenses, subscriptions, services, and implementation obligations. These businesses often enter into complex arrangements with multiple deliverables, variable pricing, renewal provisions, customer acceptance terms, and usage-based fees. Warning signs include rapid growth in deferred revenue without a corresponding operational explanation, unusual contract modifications near period-end, side letters affecting pricing or cancellation rights, and aggressive assumptions about when performance obligations have been satisfied. Auditors should question large increases in capitalized software assets, especially when the company is under earnings pressure. Another industry-specific concern is whether reported recurring revenue metrics align with underlying contracts and billing patterns. If management highlights strong subscription growth while cash collections, churn data, or customer retention metrics tell a different story, revenue quality may be weaker than presented. In technology entities, the pace of product change also increases the risk of impairment and obsolescence in capitalized assets and acquired intangibles.

EXAMPLE

During the audit of a cloud software company, the auditor reviewed a surge in fourth-quarter revenue and noticed several contracts signed in the final week of the year. Management stated that the increase reflected strong subscription demand, yet cash collections had not risen at the same pace and churn reports showed that renewals were weakening. Several of the new agreements bundled software access, implementation services, training, and future customization work, but the accounting team had recognized a large portion of the revenue immediately upon contract execution.

When the auditor examined the contracts more closely, additional concerns emerged. Two agreements had side letters granting extended cancellation rights, and one major customer arrangement had been modified just before year-end to change pricing and add service obligations. Management argued that these changes were routine, but the underlying documentation suggested that not all performance obligations had been satisfied. At the same time, the company had capitalized a significant amount of software development cost even though one product line was facing declining usage and possible replacement by a newer platform.

The auditor also compared management's reported recurring revenue growth to billing records and retention data. The metrics presented to investors emphasized subscription expansion, but actual billing patterns showed heavier discounting and shorter customer commitments. Taken together, these issues suggested possible premature revenue recognition, overly aggressive capitalization of development costs, and potential impairment risk for capitalized software assets.

In financial institutions, red flags often relate to loan quality, allowance estimates, the valuation of financial instruments, liquidity pressure, and regulatory compliance. Banks, credit unions, and similar entities operate in an environment where relatively small changes in credit assumptions can have large effects on earnings and capital. Warning signs include unusually low loan loss provisions relative to delinquency trends, rapid growth in higher-risk lending categories, concentrations in vulnerable industries or geographic areas, and repeated restructurings of troubled loans without clear evidence of improved borrower performance. Fair value issues are also significant, particularly when securities or derivatives are valued using less observable inputs. Auditors should be alert when marks remain stable despite market volatility or when management relies heavily on internally developed models without strong validation. Liquidity red flags include rising dependence on wholesale funding, deteriorating deposit stability, or off-balance-sheet commitments not fully reflected in risk assessments. In this industry, regulatory matters are especially relevant. Examination findings, compliance deficiencies, and capital adequacy concerns can signal broader financial reporting risk, even if the immediate issue appears operational or supervisory.

EXAMPLE

During the audit of a regional bank, the auditor noted that the allowance for credit losses had remained nearly unchanged from the prior quarter even though delinquencies in commercial real estate loans had increased and several borrowers had requested modified payment terms. Management explained that the borrowers were expected to recover and that collateral values remained strong. However, loan files showed repeated renewals and restructurings for some troubled credits, with limited evidence that the borrowers' cash flow had actually improved.

The auditor also identified rapid growth in construction lending within one metropolitan area where vacancy rates were rising. Despite that concentration risk, the bank's loss provision remained modest. At the same time, the valuation of certain mortgage-backed securities had not changed significantly, even though comparable market data indicated increased volatility. Management relied on internal valuation models, but the documentation of model validation and key assumptions was incomplete.

Liquidity pressures added to the concern. Deposit balances had declined, and the bank was relying more heavily on short-term wholesale borrowings to fund operations. In addition, recent regulatory correspondence described weaknesses in credit administration and risk grading practices. Management treated those findings as routine supervisory matters, but the auditor viewed them as relevant to its financial reporting.

Taken together, these issues suggested the possible understatement of credit losses, questionable fair value measurements, and increased risk related to liquidity and regulatory compliance.

In nonprofit entities, red flags often involve donor restrictions, grant compliance, allocation of expenses, and the classification of contributions and exchange transactions. Nonprofits may face pressure to demonstrate program efficiency and stewardship, which can create incentives to understate administrative costs or classify restricted funds improperly. Warning signs include vague tracking of donor restrictions, releases from restriction without clear support, grants recognized before eligibility requirements are met, and cost allocations that shift too much expense into program services. Auditors should also watch for weaknesses in oversight where boards are highly mission-focused but less attentive to financial controls. Related-party issues may arise in smaller nonprofits where founders, board members, or affiliated entities have significant operational influence. Since many nonprofits rely on grants and contributions, going concern and compliance risks can also become significant if funding sources are concentrated or conditional.

EXAMPLE

During the audit of a community health nonprofit, the auditor noted that a large grant had been recognized as revenue before year-end even though the grant agreement required the organization to complete specific outreach milestones first. Management stated that the work was substantially underway and that funding was expected, but could not provide documentation showing that the eligibility conditions had actually been met. At the same time, several donor-restricted contributions had been released from restriction and moved into operating revenue, yet the supporting schedules did not clearly show that the restricted purposes had been satisfied.

The auditor also reviewed the statement of functional expenses and found that a high percentage of salaries, occupancy costs, and administrative support had been allocated to program services rather than management and general activities. When asked how the allocations were determined, management provided broad descriptions but little contemporaneous support. The allocation percentages had also changed noticeably from the prior year without a clear operational reason.

Further inquiry revealed that a board member owned a consulting firm that had been paid to manage a fundraising campaign. The relationship had been disclosed informally, but no formal conflict review appeared in the board minutes. In addition, the nonprofit depended heavily on two major grantors whose renewals were uncertain.

These issues suggested possible improper revenue recognition, weak tracking of donor restrictions, aggressive expense allocation, related-party governance concerns, and heightened going concern risk.

In governmental audits, red flags often relate to compliance with laws and regulations, budgetary control, grant spending, and fund accounting. Governmental entities may have complex restrictions on how resources can be used, and misstatements can arise not only from accounting errors but also from noncompliance that affects financial reporting or required disclosures. Warning signs include recurring budget overruns, interfund balances that remain unsettled, expenditures charged to grants near the end of the funding period without persuasive support, and weak controls over procurement or payroll. Governments may also face pressure to defer maintenance, delay the recognition of obligations, or use one-time financing sources to close budget gaps while presenting operations as stable. Auditors should be attentive to the relationship between budgetary results, fund balance trends, and legal spending authority. A government that appears balanced only because of unusual transfers, delayed payments, or short-term borrowing may carry red flags that affect both accounting and compliance conclusions.

EXAMPLE

During the audit of a midsized city, the auditor noted that the general fund reported a small year-end surplus even though several departments had exceeded their original budgets. Management explained that the city had controlled spending carefully, but the budget-to-actual reports showed large transfers from utility and capital project funds late in the year. In addition, interfund receivables and payables had remained outstanding for many months with little evidence of settlement. The auditor also found that road repair invoices relating to work completed before year-end were recorded in the following period, which reduced current-year expenditures. These items suggested that the city's balanced presentation might depend on timing shifts and unusual financing measures rather than sustainable operations.

The auditor also reviewed a federal grant that was about to expire and found a spike in grant-charged expenditures during the final month of the funding period. Several payroll charges and supply purchases had weak supporting documentation, and procurement files showed exceptions to competitive bidding requirements. When questioned, department personnel gave inconsistent explanations about whether the costs were truly grant-related. The city had also used short-term tax anticipation borrowing to cover cash needs while publicly describing its finances as stable. Taken together, the recurring budget overruns, delayed recognition of obligations, unsettled interfund balances, questionable grant charges, and weak procurement controls represented important red flags affecting both compliance and financial reporting.

In healthcare organizations, red flags often arise in revenue recognition, contractual allowances, third-party reimbursements, physician arrangements, and regulatory compliance. Healthcare billing is highly complex, with revenue depending on payer contracts, coding practices, denials, adjustments, and estimates of amounts collectible from insurers and patients. Warning signs include significant changes in net patient service revenue without similar changes in volume or case mix, unstable allowance methodologies, large aged receivables from payers, and unusual trends in denials or appeals. Auditors should also be alert to compliance-related red flags involving government reimbursement programs, since improper billing, unsupported coding, or a failure to meet regulatory requirements can create both financial misstatement and legal exposure. Relationships with physicians, management service organizations, and affiliated clinics may also present related-party or non-arm's-length concerns. In addition, healthcare entities often face impairment issues related to facilities, service lines, or acquired practices if reimbursement pressure or patient demand changes significantly. Because estimates are central to healthcare revenue, analytical consistency between admissions, procedures, payer mix, cash collections, and reported revenue is especially important.

EXAMPLE

During the audit of a regional hospital system, the auditor noted that net patient service revenue had increased significantly from the prior year even though admissions and outpatient procedure volume had remained relatively stable. Management attributed the increase to improved reimbursement and better collections, but supporting trends were inconsistent. Accounts receivable aging showed a growing balance of older claims from major insurers, denial rates had risen, and cash collections had not increased in proportion to reported revenue. The methodology used to estimate contractual allowances had also changed during the year, yet management could not clearly explain why the revised assumptions were more appropriate.

Additional concerns arose when the auditor reviewed selected billing and compliance matters. Several high-dollar claims to government programs involved coding levels that were more aggressive than in prior periods, and a number of appealed denials had been recorded as receivables even though collection remained uncertain. The hospital also had a financial arrangement with a physician group that provided management services to an affiliated clinic, and the terms appeared more favorable than typical market arrangements. At the same time, one recently acquired specialty practice continued to report losses because patient demand had fallen below expectations, but no impairment analysis had been prepared.

These conditions suggested the possible overstatement of revenue and receivables, weaknesses in allowance estimates, compliance risk in reimbursement practices, related-party concerns, and potential impairment issues.

These industry-specific red flags are important because they help auditors move beyond a generic checklist approach. A condition that seems ordinary in one industry may be highly unusual in another. For example, large deferred revenue balances may be expected in software subscriptions but less so in certain manufacturing settings. Inventory obsolescence may develop quickly in retail fashion but more gradually in industrial supply businesses. Claims revenue may be common in construction but not in routine service contracts. The auditor must therefore understand the economic logic of the industry well enough to recognize when management's accounting treatment does not fit normal operating patterns.

Industry-specific red flags also tend to cluster. A software company with aggressive revenue recognition may also capitalize development costs aggressively. A manufacturer with weak inventory controls may also show unusual margins and outdated overhead assumptions. A financial institution with understated credit losses may also face liquidity stress and regulatory findings. A healthcare provider with volatile reimbursement estimates may also have compliance exposure. Because of this, auditors should interpret red flags in the context of the full industry risk profile rather than as isolated symptoms.

A careful industry-based assessment strengthens audit quality by making risk identification more realistic and more targeted. Red flags in manufacturing, retail, construction, software, financial institutions, nonprofits, governments, and healthcare organizations each reflect the unique pressures and accounting judgments common to those sectors. When auditors understand those patterns, they are better able to challenge explanations that sound reasonable only because they are wrapped in industry jargon or complexity. Industry knowledge does not replace professional skepticism. It sharpens it by helping the auditor distinguish between what is normal for the sector and what may indicate a material misstatement hidden within routine operations.

Auditor Responses to Red Flags

Identifying a red flag is only the beginning of the auditor's responsibility. A warning sign has little value unless it leads to a thoughtful and proportionate audit response. Red flags do not automatically prove fraud or material misstatement, but they do indicate that the original audit approach may no longer be sufficient. An effective auditor responds by reassessing risk, strengthening procedures, and seeking more persuasive evidence. The purpose of that response is not to punish management for unusual conditions or to assume misconduct without basis. Rather, it is to ensure that the audit remains aligned with the actual level of risk revealed during the engagement. If the auditor observes suspicious transactions, weak controls, inconsistent explanations, or unusual analytical relationships and then continues with the original audit plan unchanged, the value of red flag identification is lost. A high-quality audit requires the auditor to translate warning signs into specific, documented actions that address the possibility of error, fraud, bias, or incomplete disclosure.

One of the most common and necessary responses is expanding substantive procedures. Substantive procedures are designed to detect material misstatements at the assertion level, and when red flags appear, those procedures often need to become broader, deeper, or more targeted. Expansion may involve testing additional transactions, examining more supporting documents, tracing items across a longer time period, or increasing the level of detail within a high-risk area. For example, if revenue cutoff issues emerge near period-end, the auditor may test a wider range of sales and shipping transactions before and after year-end rather than relying on a smaller planned sample. If unusual inventory adjustments appear, the auditor may examine more journal entries, perform additional physical count procedures, or reconcile a larger set of inventory records to source documents. The key principle is that the nature and extent of audit work should match the level of concern. A red flag indicates that ordinary procedures may not be sufficient to address the identified risk. Expanding substantive work helps the auditor move beyond surface explanations and obtain more direct evidence about whether the financial statements are materially misstated.

Another important response is revising risk assessments. Audit planning begins with a preliminary assessment of where misstatements are likely to occur, but risk assessment is not static. As the audit progresses, the auditor may learn new information that changes the understanding of the entity, its internal controls, its incentives, or its financial reporting behavior. A red flag often means that the original risk assessment was incomplete, too optimistic, or no longer current. For example, evidence of management override, inconsistent documentation, or a weakened control environment may require the auditor to increase the assessed risk of material misstatement in one or more areas. That change can affect not only specific accounts, but also the overall audit strategy. Revising risk assessments is critical because it ensures that the audit remains responsive to actual conditions rather than being tied to earlier assumptions. If the auditor identifies heightened risk but fails to update the formal risk assessment, the audit approach may become inconsistent with the evidence gathered. A disciplined auditor treats red flags as potential indicators that the entire risk profile of the engagement needs to be reconsidered.

EXAMPLE

During the audit of a wholesale distributor, the auditor initially assessed revenue recognition as a moderate risk area because the company had a history of stable operations and no significant prior-year issues. As fieldwork progressed, however, several red flags emerged. The auditor found unusual sales recorded in the final days of the year, including large shipments to a small number of customers with extended payment terms. Customer confirmations revealed disputes about quantities received, and internal emails suggested that some shipments had been pushed out to meet quarterly targets. In addition, management responses to questions about return rights and side agreements were vague and inconsistent.

These findings caused the auditor to reconsider the original risk assessment. What had first appeared to be routine year-end activity now suggested a heightened risk of cutoff errors, premature revenue recognition, and possible management override. The auditor concluded that the previous assessment had been too low because it had relied heavily on management's description of controls and on past experience rather than on current-year evidence. As a result, the auditor increased the assessed risk of material misstatement for revenue and receivables and also reconsidered the broader control environment.

That revision affected the audit strategy. The auditor expanded substantive testing, increased sample sizes, performed more detailed cutoff procedures, reviewed additional contracts, and placed less reliance on internal controls. Revising the risk assessment ensured that the audit response matched the actual level of risk indicated by the evidence.

Increasing sample sizes is another common response when red flags suggest that a population may contain more exceptions than originally expected. Sampling is based on the assumption that a properly selected subset of items can provide evidence about the larger population. When unusual transactions, control failures, or inconsistencies are found, that assumption may still hold, but the original sample size may no longer provide a sufficient basis for conclusion. A larger sample can improve the auditor's ability to detect whether an identified issue is isolated or part of a broader pattern. For example, if duplicate payments are found in an initial disbursement test, the auditor may expand the sample to determine whether the problem is limited to one vendor or reflects a systemic accounts payable weakness. If several customer confirmations reveal disputed balances, the auditor may confirm more receivables to assess the extent of the issue. Increasing sample size is not a mechanical solution to every red flag, but it is often an appropriate response when the concern involves frequency, pervasiveness, or the reliability of a process across a broader population.

In more serious cases, the auditor may need to use forensic-style procedures. These are not limited to formal forensic engagements. Rather, they involve a more investigative, less predictable, and more skeptical approach to testing when ordinary audit techniques may not be enough. Forensic-style procedures often focus on intentional concealment, unusual patterns, and evidence that may not appear in routine transaction testing. Examples include detailed journal entry analysis, review of deleted or adjusted transactions, examination of unusual user activity in information systems, tracing funds through bank accounts, searching for related-party connections, or looking for hidden side agreements and off-record communications. The use of these procedures becomes especially important when fraud risk rises, when management explanations lack credibility, or when documentation appears manipulated or incomplete. A standard audit approach may detect ordinary errors, but intentional misconduct often requires more pointed and less predictable testing. Forensic-style work is particularly valuable because it recognizes that a party engaged in fraud may also be engaged in concealment. Therefore, the response must focus not only on whether a balance is reasonable, but on whether someone may have structured records or transactions to avoid normal detection.

EXAMPLE

During the audit of a consumer products company, the auditor became concerned about possible fraudulent revenue recognition after identifying several large period-end sales with unusual terms. Management insisted the transactions were valid, but supporting documents were incomplete, customer confirmations were delayed, and some invoices had been revised shortly after year-end. Ordinary substantive testing showed inconsistencies, but not enough to explain whether the issue was error or intentional concealment. Because the pattern suggested possible manipulation, the auditor expanded the work to include forensic-style procedures.

The auditor performed a detailed journal entry analysis focused on manual entries posted late at night, near period-end, and by senior accounting personnel. Several entries moved revenue between accounts without clear explanation. System logs showed that shipping dates on certain transactions had been changed after the initial entry, and deleted order records were recovered from the system archive. The auditor also reviewed email traffic and found side communications between sales managers and accounting staff discussing how to "hold the number" until quarter-end. Bank tracing revealed that one supposed customer payment had come from an entity with ties to a company executive rather than from the customer itself. Further background review showed that the customer was related to a former executive through a privately owned affiliate.

These procedures provided evidence not just of questionable balances, but of deliberate efforts to structure transactions and records to avoid normal audit detection.

Seeking corroborating external evidence is another critical response to red flags. When internal records and management explanations become less reliable, the auditor should place greater weight on evidence obtained from independent outside sources. External evidence often provides stronger support because it is less subject to management influence and may directly confirm the existence, amount, terms, or condition of an item. Examples include customer confirmations, vendor statements, bank confirmations, legal letters, third-party warehouse confirmations, public filings, lender correspondence, and external market data. If management asserts that a receivable is collectible despite a slow payment history, subsequent cash receipts or direct customer confirmation may provide more persuasive evidence than internal aging schedules. If inventory is held at a third-party location, confirmation from the custodian is often more reliable than internal listings alone. Corroborating evidence is especially important when the red flag involves disputed facts, weak internal documentation, or possible bias in management-produced information. A careful auditor recognizes that when internal evidence becomes questionable, the answer is not simply to request more of the same type of evidence. It is to look outward for independent confirmation.

Involving specialists or senior personnel is also an appropriate response when red flags exceed the experience, authority, or technical expertise of the original audit team. Some warning signs raise issues that require specialized knowledge, such as fair value measurement, information technology controls, tax exposures, legal contingencies, fraud indicators, or complex contract interpretation. Other situations may call for more senior judgment because the red flag involves management integrity, materiality-sensitive decisions, or significant changes to audit scope. For example, unusual system override activity may require the involvement of an IT audit specialist. A questionable valuation model may warrant assistance from a valuation expert. Evidence suggesting intentional manipulation may require consultation with fraud specialists or senior engagement leadership. Involving more experienced personnel is also important because it reduces the risk that significant warning signs will be minimized or misunderstood by staff who are too close to the day-to-day work or who lack the confidence to challenge management aggressively. Red flags should not be managed at the lowest level possible simply for efficiency. They should be elevated when the seriousness or complexity of the issue requires broader expertise or stronger oversight.

These responses often work best in combination rather than alone. A red flag involving revenue recognition may require revised risk assessments, expanded substantive testing, larger samples, more customer confirmations, and involvement of senior team members. A suspected control override may lead to forensic-style procedures, IT specialist involvement, and more extensive external corroboration. A questionable estimate may require additional substantive work, revised risk evaluation, and the use of a specialist. The right response depends on the nature of the red flag, the assertion affected, and the possibility that the issue reflects a broader pattern rather than an isolated exception.

The most important principle is that auditor responses must be intentional, documented, and proportionate. A red flag should lead to a clear explanation of what changed in the audit approach and why. It is not enough to note the concern in workpapers without adjusting the substance of the audit. Nor is it enough to perform extra work without linking that work to the risk being addressed. Effective responses show that the auditor understood the warning sign, evaluated its implications, and designed procedures specifically to resolve the uncertainty it created.

In the end, red flags test the auditor's judgment as much as the client's accounting. The question is not simply whether the auditor noticed the warning sign. It is whether the auditor responded in a way that meaningfully reduced the risk of issuing an inappropriate opinion. Expanding substantive procedures, revising risk assessments, increasing sample sizes, applying forensic-style methods, seeking external corroboration, and involving specialists or senior personnel are all tools that help the auditor move from suspicion to evidence-based conclusion. Their proper use is essential to an audit that is both skeptical and reliable.

Documentation of Red Flags

The identification of a red flag is only useful if it is documented clearly, evaluated thoughtfully, and connected to an appropriate audit response. In every audit, unusual conditions, inconsistent explanations, weak controls, and suspicious transactions may emerge during planning, testing, inquiry, or review. If those matters are not documented properly, the audit file may fail to show how the team recognized the issue, why it mattered, what was done in response, and whether the matter was resolved satisfactorily. Good documentation is therefore an essential part of audit quality. It supports supervision and review, helps demonstrate compliance with auditing standards, preserves the reasoning behind key judgments, and allows the audit team to distinguish between minor irregularities and matters that may indicate material misstatement or fraud. Red flag documentation is not just a clerical exercise. It is part of the process by which the auditor transforms concern into evidence-based judgment.

A starting point is recording identified red flags in the workpapers in a way that is specific, factual, and understandable. A vague note such as "unusual transaction noted" or "issue with controls" is rarely sufficient. The workpaper should describe what the red flag was, when it arose, what evidence gave rise to the concern, and what account, transaction class, process, or disclosure area it affected. For example, instead of stating that revenue appeared unusual, the auditor should document that sales in the final three business days of the year increased significantly compared to prior periods and that several of those transactions involved extended payment terms not seen in the standard customer contract. This level of precision matters because it allows reviewers and team members to understand the nature of the concern without relying on memory or informal conversation. Clear documentation also helps prevent red flags from being minimized over time. A matter that seemed important when first identified can appear less significant later if it is not captured accurately in the file. The workpaper should therefore record the facts giving rise to the concern, not just a general impression that something seemed unusual.

EXAMPLE

During the audit of a retailer, the auditor did not simply note that revenue looked unusual. Instead, the workpaper stated that sales recorded during the final three business days of the year were 34 percent higher than the average for the preceding monthly period and 29 percent higher than the same three-day period in the prior year. The workpaper also noted that eight of the fifteen largest year-end sales included payment terms of 120 days, whereas standard terms were 30 days. Supporting evidence cited in the workpaper included the sales register, selected customer invoices, contract summaries, and aging reports. The auditor further documented that the affected area was revenue recognition and accounts receivable, with possible implications for cutoff and collectability assertions. By recording the exact nature of the red flag, the timing, the supporting evidence, and the accounts involved, the workpaper allowed reviewers to understand why the issue mattered and why additional audit procedures were necessary.

It is equally important to link red flags to the relevant audit assertions. A red flag becomes more meaningful when the auditor explains exactly what type of misstatement risk it may indicate. Auditing is not simply about noticing unusual events. It is about understanding how those events could affect the fairness of the financial statements. A red flag may relate to existence, completeness, valuation, cutoff, rights and obligations, or presentation and disclosure. For example, disputed receivable balances may suggest valuation risk, but they may also raise questions about existence or revenue cutoff. Inventory stored at a third-party location may affect existence and rights. A late journal entry reducing accrued liabilities may indicate completeness and cutoff concerns. By linking the red flag to one or more assertions, the auditor shows why the issue matters and how it fits into the broader risk assessment framework. This also helps ensure that the response is properly targeted. If the red flag is documented only as a general concern, the follow-up work may become unfocused. Assertion-based documentation sharpens both the reasoning and the resulting procedures.

Once a red flag has been identified and linked to assertions, the next step is documenting the follow-up procedures performed in response. This part of the file should show how the auditor addressed the concern, not merely that the concern existed. The documentation should identify what additional steps were taken, why those steps were selected, what evidence was obtained, and how that evidence was evaluated. For example, if unusual credit memos issued after period-end created concern about revenue recognition, the workpapers should indicate whether the auditor expanded sales cutoff testing, examined customer correspondence, reviewed return activity, confirmed balances, or analyzed subsequent cash receipts. If the issue involved management override, the file should show whether the auditor performed additional journal entry testing, reviewed approvals, assessed user access, or consulted more senior personnel. Good documentation does not simply list procedures. It explains the connection between the red flag and the work performed. This is important because it demonstrates that the audit response was not random or routine, but specifically designed to address the identified risk. It also gives reviewers a basis for evaluating whether the response was sufficient.

EXAMPLE

During the audit of a distributor, the auditor identified a red flag when an unusual volume of credit memos was issued in the first two weeks after year-end. The workpaper did not merely note the existence of the credit memos. It explained that the pattern raised concern about possible premature revenue recognition and cutoff errors. In response, the auditor expanded the testing of year-end sales transactions, selected a larger sample of shipments from the final week of the reporting period, and traced them to shipping documents, customer orders, invoices, and subsequent credit memos. The auditor also reviewed customer email correspondence for evidence of return rights or shipment disputes, confirmed selected receivable balances, and examined subsequent cash receipts. The workpaper documented that these procedures were chosen because they directly addressed whether recorded sales were valid, final, and collectable. It then summarized the results, noting which transactions were supported, which exceptions were found, and why the evidence suggested that additional review of revenue recognition was necessary.

Another key element is evaluating whether the issue was actually resolved. Auditors often perform additional procedures after identifying a red flag, but the workpaper should go beyond describing the steps taken. It should state the conclusion reached and explain whether the evidence obtained reduced the concern, confirmed the issue, or left uncertainty unresolved. This evaluation requires judgment. In some cases, the red flag may be explained satisfactorily by persuasive evidence. In others, the additional work may reveal that the problem is broader than first believed. Sometimes the issue cannot be fully resolved, in which case the auditor may need to modify the risk assessment further, expand testing again, communicate the issue upward, or consider the implications for the opinion. The documentation should reflect this reasoning clearly. A file that lists extra procedures without stating whether the underlying concern was resolved does not provide a complete audit trail. The purpose of red flag documentation is not only to show activity, but to show how the auditor arrived at a conclusion about the significance of the matter.

The final step is communicating red flag conclusions clearly within the audit documentation and, where appropriate, through formal audit communications. The workpapers should summarize the issue in a way that allows engagement leaders, reviewers, and future team members to understand what happened and why it mattered. This is especially important when the red flag affects planning decisions, control reliance, fraud considerations, communications with governance, or judgments about materiality and financial statement presentation. Clear communication within the file should include the nature of the red flag, the assertions affected, the procedures performed, the results obtained, the conclusion reached, and any remaining concerns. If the matter was significant enough to be discussed with management, those charged with governance, specialists, or legal counsel, that communication should also be documented appropriately. The goal is to create a coherent record that explains the issue from identification through conclusion. A reviewer should be able to understand not only that a red flag existed, but also whether it was isolated, whether it indicated a larger pattern, and how it influenced the final audit approach.

Strong documentation of red flags serves several purposes at once. It supports professional skepticism by forcing the auditor to articulate why something appeared unusual and whether the explanation was truly satisfactory. It supports review by making the team's reasoning transparent. It supports accountability by showing that concerns were investigated rather than ignored. It also supports continuity, since future audit teams may look back at prior-year red flag documentation to identify recurring issues, management behavior patterns, or control weaknesses that remain relevant. A matter that appears minor in one year may become more significant when seen as part of a repeated pattern over time.

In practice, the quality of red flag documentation often reflects the quality of the audit itself. A weak file may show scattered concerns, incomplete responses, and unclear conclusions. A strong file shows disciplined thinking. It records the facts, links them to assertions, documents the response, evaluates the results, and communicates the conclusion clearly. That process is essential because audits frequently turn on the handling of matters that were not routine. Red flags are exactly those matters. If they are not documented well, the audit may fail to show that the most important issues were recognized and addressed with the seriousness they required.

Communication of Red Flags

The value of identifying an auditing red flag depends heavily on what happens after it is recognized. A warning sign that remains with one staff member, is discussed only informally, or is explained away without broader evaluation can easily become the starting point for audit failure. Communication and escalation are therefore essential parts of the audit response. They ensure that unusual conditions are shared with the right people, evaluated at the proper level of authority, and addressed in a way that reflects their seriousness. Effective communication also helps the audit team avoid fragmentation, where different individuals observe different parts of the same problem without connecting them. When red flags involve possible misstatement, control failure, or fraud, the audit process must include timely internal discussion, appropriate external communication, and careful consideration of legal and regulatory responsibilities. The issue is not merely whether something suspicious was noticed. It is whether it was communicated clearly enough, and escalated appropriately enough, to allow a sound audit judgment.

A first priority is communicating issues within the audit team. Audit engagements are often performed by multiple people across different workstreams, locations, and levels of seniority. One person may identify an unusual journal entry, another may encounter conflicting explanations from management, and another may notice inconsistent analytical results. If these observations are not shared, the team may fail to recognize that they point to a broader pattern of risk. Internal communication therefore needs to be intentional and continuous, not limited to formal planning meetings. Staff should understand that raising concerns is part of audit quality, not a sign of inefficiency or inexperience. Seniors and managers should create an environment in which team members feel comfortable escalating unusual findings without fear that they are overreacting. This is especially important when the issue involves management behavior, questionable documentation, or a matter that seems small in isolation but may be significant in combination with other evidence. Internal communication should include what was observed, why it appears unusual, which assertions may be affected, and whether additional procedures may be needed. When the team communicates well, red flags are more likely to be seen as interconnected evidence rather than as isolated exceptions scattered through the workpapers.

The next step is discussing concerns with management. In many cases, the auditor should give management an opportunity to explain unusual transactions, documentation gaps, inconsistent reports, or control breakdowns before drawing firm conclusions. This discussion is important because some red flags have legitimate explanations, and management may provide relevant operational context, supporting records, or corrective actions that were not visible initially. However, the purpose of the discussion is not simply to accept reassurance. It is to evaluate whether management's explanation is responsive, credible, and supported by evidence. The tone of these conversations also matters. Auditors should be direct and professional, focusing on facts, inconsistencies, and the need for clarification rather than making premature accusations. At the same time, the auditor should not soften the issue so much that management fails to understand its seriousness. If the concern involves a high-risk area such as revenue recognition, related-party transactions, or possible management override, the discussion may need to occur with more senior members of management rather than with process-level personnel alone. Management responses should then be assessed in light of the broader audit evidence. A plausible verbal explanation is not enough if the documentation, system data, or third-party evidence points in a different direction.

Some matters go beyond management discussion and must be reported to those charged with governance. This group typically includes the audit committee, board of directors, or an equivalent body responsible for overseeing financial reporting, internal control, and management accountability. Governance communication becomes especially important when the red flag involves significant deficiencies or material weaknesses in internal control, suspected fraud, management integrity concerns, aggressive accounting judgments, or unresolved disputes between management and the auditor. The reason for this escalation is straightforward. Those charged with governance need to understand significant risks affecting the financial statements and the conduct of the audit, particularly when the matter involves individuals within management who may not be objective in evaluating themselves. Effective reporting to governance should be clear, specific, and balanced. It should explain the nature of the issue, the procedures performed, what remains unresolved, and why the matter is significant. If the auditor communicates only in vague or overly technical language, governance bodies may not appreciate the seriousness of the concern. Good governance communication helps ensure that red flags receive oversight at the appropriate level and that management is not left as the sole interpreter of issues that may reflect on its own conduct.

Escalating suspected fraud requires special care and discipline because fraud concerns can quickly affect the scope, direction, and even the continuation of the engagement. Not every red flag indicates fraud, but when the possibility becomes credible, the auditor must move beyond routine issue resolution and treat the matter with heightened skepticism and control over communication. Fraud escalation usually begins internally, with prompt discussion among senior engagement team members and, where appropriate, firm specialists. The team must consider the nature of the suspected conduct, who may be involved, how the issue could affect the financial statements, and whether existing procedures remain adequate. If fraud may involve employees below senior management, the matter is typically communicated to an appropriate level of management and those charged with governance. If fraud may involve senior management, the issue may need to bypass management and go directly to the audit committee or equivalent governance body. This distinction matters because communication to implicated individuals may compromise the audit response, enable concealment, or interfere with evidence preservation.

EXAMPLE

During the audit of a manufacturing company, the auditor identified several manual journal entries posted late at night near year-end that increased revenue and reduced reserves. Initial explanations from the accounting department were inconsistent, and supporting documentation was incomplete. Because the pattern suggested possible intentional manipulation rather than ordinary error, the engagement partner was informed immediately, and the matter was discussed with senior team members and a forensic specialist. The team considered who had access to post the entries, which financial statement areas were affected, and whether additional procedures were needed to preserve evidence and evaluate management override.

Because the entries appeared to have been approved by the chief financial officer, the auditor did not raise the matter through normal management channels. Instead, the concern was communicated directly to the audit committee chair. This approach reduced the risk that an implicated individual could alter records, coordinate stories, or obstruct the investigation. The escalation changed the audit response from routine follow-up to controlled fraud-oriented procedures.

The escalation of suspected fraud also requires the auditor to think carefully about documentation, confidentiality, and further evidence gathering. The team may need to involve forensic specialists, expand journal entry testing, obtain more external corroboration, or reduce predictability in procedures. Communications should be controlled so that only those who need to know are informed, especially in the early stages when facts are still developing. At the same time, the seriousness of the matter should not be minimized. A delayed or hesitant escalation can allow the suspected conduct to continue or make later investigation more difficult. Fraud concerns often place the auditor in a difficult position because the client relationship may become strained and management may respond defensively. Even so, the auditor's duty is to respond to the evidence, not to preserve convenience. When suspected fraud arises, escalation is not optional. It is a core part of protecting the integrity of the audit.

Legal and regulatory reporting considerations add another layer to communication and escalation decisions. Auditors generally owe duties of confidentiality to the client, but those duties may be limited by professional standards, laws, regulations, or specific reporting obligations depending on the type of entity and the nature of the issue. For example, certain industries may require communication with regulators when financial reporting irregularities, compliance failures, or illegal acts are identified. Public company audits can involve specific governance communication requirements and, in some circumstances, implications for regulatory filings or auditor resignation decisions. Governmental, financial institution, and healthcare audits may also carry special reporting expectations tied to public funding, supervisory authorities, or compliance frameworks. Even when external reporting is not immediately required, the auditor must consider whether unresolved issues affect the audit opinion, internal control reporting, required communications, or the ability to continue the engagement. Legal counsel may need to be consulted when the issue involves possible illegal acts, litigation exposure, client obstruction, or uncertainty about the auditor's reporting obligations. These matters should not be handled informally. They require structured evaluation because misjudging legal or regulatory responsibilities can create significant consequences for both the client and the audit firm.

Communication and escalation are therefore not peripheral administrative steps. They are central to how an auditor turns red flags into responsible action. Internal team communication ensures that warning signs are connected and evaluated collectively. Management discussion allows explanation and challenge. Governance reporting ensures appropriate oversight. Fraud escalation protects the audit when intentional misconduct may be involved. Legal and regulatory analysis ensures that professional obligations are met beyond the immediate client relationship. A well-executed audit depends not only on finding unusual matters, but on making sure those matters are heard, understood, and elevated to the right level at the right time.

Professional Judgement

Professional judgment and professional skepticism are central to the auditor's ability to recognize and respond to red flags. Auditing standards do not expect the auditor to approach every transaction with suspicion, but they do require a questioning mind and a disciplined evaluation of evidence. Red flags matter only if the auditor is willing to notice them, interpret them correctly, and follow them to a reasoned conclusion. That process depends heavily on judgment. The same fact pattern can be dismissed as routine by one auditor and recognized as a meaningful warning sign by another. Skepticism helps bridge that difference by encouraging the auditor to pause before accepting appearances, to consider whether evidence is consistent and persuasive, and to remain alert to conditions suggesting possible misstatement due to error or fraud. In practice, the quality of an audit often depends less on whether the auditor encountered red flags and more on whether the auditor exercised sound judgment in evaluating what those warning signs meant.

One of the first challenges in this area is recognizing bias in audit judgments. Auditors, like all professionals, are vulnerable to cognitive bias. They may unconsciously favor evidence that supports an initial conclusion, trust management more readily when prior interactions have been positive, or give excessive weight to information that confirms what they expected to find. These tendencies can be especially dangerous when evaluating red flags, because warning signs often emerge gradually and may be easy to rationalize if they conflict with the auditor's early impressions of the client. For example, an auditor who begins the engagement believing that management is highly competent and honest may interpret unusual journal entries or aggressive estimates as technical issues rather than as possible indicators of bias or manipulation. Similarly, auditors may anchor too heavily on preliminary materiality judgments, prior-year results, or initial explanations and fail to adjust their thinking when new facts emerge. Recognizing bias requires self-awareness and a willingness to revisit assumptions. The auditor must ask not only whether management's explanation seems plausible, but also whether the explanation is being accepted because it is truly persuasive or because it fits comfortably with what the auditor already believed.

EXAMPLE

During the audit of a medical supply company, the auditor began the engagement with a favorable view of management because prior audits had been clean and the chief executive officer had a strong reputation for transparency. Early in fieldwork, the auditor noticed several manual journal entries posted near year-end that reduced expenses and increased reported earnings. Management explained that the entries were routine accrual adjustments needed to reflect updated information. Because that explanation was consistent with the auditor's initial positive impression, the entries were not challenged aggressively at first.

As the audit continued, additional warning signs appeared. Forecasts used to support inventory valuation seemed optimistic, and post-year-end results showed weaker sales than management had projected. The auditor also learned that one of the expense reductions related to a reserve that had been released without clear supporting analysis. Even then, the auditor was inclined to view each issue separately as a technical matter rather than as part of a broader pattern. After discussing the situation with a senior team member, the auditor reconsidered whether prior assumptions were influencing her judgment. That reflection led to expanded testing of journal entries, reserve calculations, and subsequent events. The additional work showed that management's estimates had been consistently biased toward improving earnings, demonstrating how initial trust had delayed the recognition of a significant red flag.

Another important principle is avoiding overreliance on prior-year conclusions. Familiarity with the client can be useful because it improves efficiency and deepens business understanding, but it can also reduce skepticism if the auditor begins to assume that current-year risks mirror prior-year experience. A conclusion reached in a previous audit is not evidence for the current audit unless the relevant conditions remain unchanged and that continuity has been verified. This is especially important in areas involving estimates, controls, related parties, revenue arrangements, and management behavior, all of which may shift from year to year in response to financial pressure or operational changes. A company that had a sound control environment in the prior year may now be facing turnover, liquidity stress, or strategic disruption that materially changes the risk profile. An estimate that was reasonable last year may be biased this year because market conditions have deteriorated. If the auditor allows prior-year conclusions to substitute for the current-year evaluation, red flags may be overlooked simply because they did not exist before. Professional judgment requires viewing each period on its own facts while using prior knowledge as context rather than as a shortcut.

Challenging management representations is another essential element of skepticism. Management representations are a necessary part of the audit, but they are not sufficient evidence for significant matters unless supported by other reliable information. Management may provide explanations for unusual results, assurances about collectability, descriptions of contract terms, or assessments of control effectiveness that appear reasonable on the surface. The auditor's responsibility is not to reject those statements automatically, but to test whether they are consistent with the underlying evidence. This is particularly important when red flags arise in areas where management has incentives to present a favorable picture, such as revenue recognition, allowances, impairment, contingencies, and going concern matters. Challenging management does not mean being argumentative or adversarial. It means asking follow-up questions, requesting corroboration, comparing statements to documents and external evidence, and evaluating whether the explanation fully addresses the issue. A skeptical auditor understands that management's confidence in an assertion is not evidence of its truth. Representations must be supported, especially when they concern matters that significantly affect the financial statements.

Responding to contradictory evidence is another area where judgment and skepticism are tested. Audits rarely produce perfectly consistent information. One document may support management's position while another raises doubt. Analytical procedures may suggest one conclusion while subsequent events suggest another. A customer confirmation may conflict with internal records. Contradictory evidence is especially important because it often signals that the issue is more complex, or more risky, than it first appeared. A weak audit approach may treat contradictory evidence as an annoyance to be explained away. A strong audit approach treats it as a reason to pause, investigate further, and determine which evidence is more reliable. The auditor should not resolve contradictions by defaulting to the most convenient explanation or the one least disruptive to the audit timeline. Instead, the auditor must assess the source, reliability, and relevance of each piece of evidence and determine whether additional procedures are needed. In many cases, red flags emerge not because one item is obviously wrong, but because two or more pieces of evidence do not fit together. Professional judgment is demonstrated by how the auditor handles that tension. Contradictions should sharpen the audit response, not be absorbed without analysis.

EXAMPLE

During the audit of a distributor, the auditor tested a large year-end sale that management claimed was complete and properly recognized as revenue. The signed sales invoice, shipping document, and entry in the sales journal all supported management's position. At first glance, the transaction appeared valid. However, the auditor then received a customer confirmation stating that the goods were still being held at the distributor's warehouse and would not be accepted until after the customer completed a facility expansion in the following month.

This contradiction could not be dismissed as a minor paperwork issue. The internal records suggested a completed sale, while the customer's direct response suggested that control of the goods had not yet transferred. Rather than accepting management's explanation that the customer was simply confused, the auditor performed additional procedures. These included reviewing the contract terms, examining email correspondence, inspecting warehouse records, and evaluating whether the arrangement was actually a bill-and-hold transaction.

The follow-up work showed that the customer had requested delayed delivery and retained a cancellation right until shipment. That evidence was more persuasive than the company's internal documents. The contradiction therefore led the auditor to conclude that revenue had likely been recognized too early.

Maintaining skepticism under deadline pressure is often one of the hardest practical challenges in auditing. Audits operate within budgets, reporting deadlines, staffing limitations, and client expectations, all of which create pressure to keep the engagement moving. In that environment, there is a natural temptation to accept plausible explanations quickly, limit follow-up work, or view red flags as isolated problems that can be closed efficiently. The danger is that time pressure can turn skepticism into a theoretical ideal rather than an operational reality. An auditor under pressure may ask fewer follow-up questions, rely too heavily on management-generated schedules, or postpone difficult issues until the final review stage, when there is even less time to investigate them properly. This is precisely when skepticism matters most. A red flag identified late in the audit may be more significant, not less, because it appears after the team has already formed preliminary conclusions. Maintaining skepticism under these conditions requires discipline. The auditor must be willing to revisit completed work, expand procedures when necessary, and resist the instinct to treat unresolved concerns as immaterial simply because addressing them is inconvenient.

This does not mean that every unusual item justifies endless investigation. Professional judgment still requires proportionality. The auditor must distinguish between issues that are minor and well explained and issues that carry real risk of material misstatement. But that judgment should be based on evidence and reasoning, not on a desire to protect the schedule. Strong engagement leadership is especially important here. Senior team members need to reinforce that raising concerns is part of the audit process, not an obstacle to efficiency. They also need to create room for escalation when staff encounter matters that do not fit the expected narrative. An audit team that is trained to prioritize completion over skepticism may technically finish on time while missing the very signals that matter most.

Professional judgment and skepticism are therefore not abstract ideals. They are the practical habits that determine whether red flags are recognized, interpreted properly, and pursued to a sound conclusion. Recognizing bias in one's own thinking, refusing to rely too heavily on prior-year comfort, challenging management assertions, confronting contradictory evidence honestly, and maintaining discipline under time pressure are all part of the auditor's responsibility. In a risk-based audit, many important issues do not announce themselves clearly. They appear as subtle inconsistencies, unusual explanations, and patterns that require interpretation. The auditor who exercises strong judgment and sustained skepticism is far more likely to detect those signals and respond effectively.

Case Studies in Auditing Red Flags

Case studies are useful because they show how red flags appear in practice rather than in isolation. In a real audit, warning signs rarely arrive as a single obvious event. They tend to emerge through patterns in documentation, analytics, inquiry responses, control weaknesses, and management behavior. The auditor's challenge is to recognize these patterns early enough to adjust the audit approach before a material misstatement goes undetected. The following case studies illustrate how red flags can develop across several audit areas and how a skeptical auditor should respond. Each example shows that the issue is not merely spotting something unusual. It is understanding why the unusual condition matters, what assertions are affected, and how the red flag should shape audit procedures and conclusions.

Revenue Fraud Case Study

A distributor of industrial components reported strong fourth-quarter sales growth even though most competitors in the same sector were experiencing declining demand. During the audit, the team noted that a substantial portion of annual revenue had been recorded in the final week of the year. The initial explanation from management was that several large customers accelerated purchases to lock in pricing before a scheduled increase. On its face, that explanation seemed plausible. However, additional red flags began to appear. Accounts receivable increased much faster than sales, several of the year-end invoices involved unusually long payment terms, and post-year-end credit memos rose sharply in January.

When the audit team reviewed supporting contracts, it found that many arrangements had been modified through email rather than formal amendments. Some emails suggested that customers could return unsold goods or delay acceptance if market demand weakened. Sales staff described these communications as normal "commercial flexibility," but they affected whether control had actually transferred and whether the revenue should have been recognized at year-end. Customer confirmations added further concern, since a few customers disputed balances or described the shipments as subject to later review.

The red flags in this case included unusual end-of-period sales volume, receivables growth inconsistent with collections, side agreements affecting finality, and excessive post-period credits. Together, these indicators suggested that the company had recognized revenue prematurely to meet its annual earnings targets. A proper auditor response would include expanded cutoff testing, review of all related correspondence, direct confirmation of transaction terms with customers, and analysis of post-period returns and collections. The central lesson is that revenue fraud often begins with a plausible business explanation, but the explanation must be tested against the economic substance of the transaction. When several red flags point in the same direction, the auditor should assume that routine revenue testing is no longer enough.

Inventory Manipulation Case Study

A manufacturer of specialty packaging materials reported a significant improvement in gross margin despite flat sales and rising raw material costs. Management attributed the margin increase to production efficiencies gained from a recent equipment upgrade. During inventory observation, however, the audit team noted several issues that did not fit that explanation. The warehouse staff had difficulty locating certain inventory items listed on count sheets, and a number of quantities required adjustment after physical counts were performed. The perpetual inventory records also showed repeated negative balances for specific product categories during the year.

Further testing revealed a pattern of large manual inventory adjustments posted late in each month, often with vague descriptions such as "true-up" or "cost correction." The company's standard costs had not been updated recently, even though material prices had changed significantly. Slow-moving finished goods remained on hand in large quantities, yet the obsolescence reserve had not increased. In addition, some inventory stored at an off-site location had not been independently confirmed for several months.

In this case, the red flags were margin results inconsistent with industry pressures, negative inventory balances, frequent manual adjustments, weak physical count reliability, and a stale reserve for obsolete goods. These factors suggested that the company may have been overstating inventory and understating the cost of sales to support reported earnings. The auditor's response should include expanded physical count procedures, testing of standard cost assumptions, review of adjustment activity by user and timing, confirmation of third-party inventory, and independent assessment of obsolescence. The case shows that inventory manipulation often does not begin with fabricated items alone. It may arise through a combination of costing assumptions, unsupported adjustments, weak count controls, and a reluctance to recognize declining value. A gross margin that looks too good can be one of the strongest red flags in the audit.

Cash Theft and Concealment Case Study

A regional service company maintained multiple bank accounts and a decentralized cash receipts process. During the audit, the team observed that bank reconciliations were often completed weeks late and contained numerous old reconciling items described only as "timing difference." The controller explained that staffing shortages had delayed the monthly close. That explanation might have been sufficient if the issue had been limited to timing, but other warning signs appeared. Several customer payments were deposited later than expected, and some receipts had been posted to accounts receivable days after the deposit date. In addition, a pattern of manual journal entries moved cash between accounts near month-end and then reversed shortly after the reporting date.

When the auditors examined customer account activity more closely, they found that receipts from one customer were being applied to the balances of another. This suggested lapping, in which one cash theft is hidden by using later receipts to cover the earlier shortage. Transfer testing also revealed potential kiting activity, since interbank transfers were recorded as deposits in one account before the corresponding disbursements cleared the other account. The company's segregation of duties was weak because the same employee handled receipt posting, bank deposit preparation, and certain reconciliation steps.

The red flags in this case included late reconciliations, vague reconciling items, delayed deposits, unusual inter-account transfers, and the misapplication of receipts. The appropriate audit response would involve expanded bank transfer testing, detailed review of receipt posting dates, confirmation of customer balances, analysis of journal entries involving cash, and evaluation of the employee's access and responsibilities. The case illustrates that cash theft often survives because the concealment mechanisms appear routine. Auditors should be especially skeptical when timing explanations are repeated, reconciliation items remain unresolved, and cash-related journal entries appear to manage balances rather than reflect real treasury activity.

Related-Party Concealment Case Study

A privately held company reported strong growth in sales to a new customer that quickly became one of its largest accounts. Management described the customer as an independent distributor entering a new regional market. During the audit, however, the team noticed that the customer's mailing address resembled that of another entity mentioned in board minutes. Further inquiry revealed that one of the company's executives had indirect ownership ties to the customer through a family trust, but this relationship had not been disclosed in the financial statements.

Additional testing showed that the customer consistently received extended payment terms, purchased unusually large quantities near period-end, and returned substantial amounts of product shortly after quarter close. The pricing on the sales was also higher than the rates offered to unrelated distributors, even though the customer took little real market risk. A review of email correspondence suggested that management expected the customer to "help smooth the quarter" by accepting product temporarily. These facts pointed to a related-party arrangement lacking arm's-length economics and possibly lacking economic substance altogether.

The red flags here included an undisclosed related party, nonstandard terms, unusual pricing, end-of-period volume spikes, and post-period returns. The audit response should include a broader search for related-party relationships, review of ownership records and legal documents, evaluation of whether the revenue transactions had substance, and reassessment of financial statement disclosure adequacy. This case demonstrates that related-party issues often surface indirectly. The auditor may first notice unusual pricing, unexpected volume, or address similarities before fully understanding the relationship. Once related-party influence is identified, the auditor must shift from a routine transaction review to a substance-over-form analysis of the entire arrangement.

Management Override Case Study

A chief financial officer regularly posted top-side journal entries late in the closing process. The entries were round-dollar amounts, affected reserves and accruals, and carried brief explanations such as "management adjustment." Accounting staff described the entries as normal. However, when asked for supporting analysis, they indicated that the CFO usually determined the amounts directly. A review of year-end entries showed that several of them increased earnings just enough to meet internal targets.

The red flags were senior management involvement, late manual entries, vague support, and a direct link to performance objectives. The auditor should respond with expanded journal entry testing, a review of estimate bias, direct challenge of the business rationale for the entries, and immediate escalation within the engagement team. This case highlights how management override can appear routine precisely because subordinates have become accustomed to it.

Going Concern Warning Signs Case Study

A healthcare services company had recurring operating losses, negative cash flow from operations, and growing dependence on short-term borrowing. During the audit, management presented optimistic forecasts showing a return to profitability, but the assumptions depended on rapid growth in patient volume and favorable reimbursement changes that had not yet occurred. At the same time, one of the company's largest referral sources had terminated its relationship.

The red flags were sustained losses, liquidity pressure, reliance on short-term financing, and forecasts unsupported by operating conditions. The auditor should test management's forecast assumptions carefully, review debt agreements and covenant status, evaluate disclosure adequacy, and consider whether substantial doubt about going concern exists. This case shows that going concern problems are often visible well before failure occurs, but only if the auditor evaluates warning signs as a connected pattern rather than as isolated financial setbacks.

These case studies demonstrate that red flags are most powerful when viewed in combination. A single unusual item may be explainable. A pattern of unusual items usually requires a different audit response. Revenue anomalies, inventory distortions, cash irregularities, concealed related-party arrangements, management override, and going concern pressures all show that the auditor's real task is not simply to notice exceptions. It is to interpret them, connect them, and respond before the financial statements become materially misleading.

Building an Audit Approach to Spot Red Flags

A strong audit does not treat red flags as isolated surprises that are addressed only when something unusual happens to appear. Instead, it builds the identification and evaluation of warning signs into the structure of the engagement from the beginning. A red-flag-oriented audit approach recognizes that material misstatements often emerge through patterns of behavior, unusual transactions, control weaknesses, and inconsistencies that may be subtle when viewed separately. The objective is not to turn every audit into a fraud investigation or to assume misconduct without evidence. The objective is to design the engagement so that the audit team is alert to signals of elevated risk and prepared to respond when those signals appear. This means integrating red flag awareness into planning, program design, staff development, data analysis, and post-engagement learning. When auditors build red flags into the way they work, they are more likely to detect issues early, allocate effort intelligently, and maintain professional skepticism throughout the audit.

The first step is embedding red flags into planning. Planning should not focus only on material account balances and routine control walkthroughs. It should also include a deliberate discussion of where warning signs are most likely to arise in the client's environment. This means considering management incentives, industry pressures, recent business changes, prior-year control problems, complex transactions, unusual accounting estimates, related-party relationships, and areas where the entity has historically struggled with documentation or close-process discipline. Red flags should be part of team brainstorming, especially in fraud discussions, because this helps the team move from abstract risk categories to practical indicators that might surface during fieldwork. For example, if the company is under lender pressure, the team should specifically consider which financial statement areas might show aggressive presentation, such as revenue, accruals, or covenant-sensitive classifications. If the client recently implemented a new system, the team should anticipate warning signs involving data inconsistencies, access control issues, or manual workarounds. Embedding red flags into planning improves the quality of the audit because it helps the team know what to look for before the evidence begins to accumulate.

The next step is designing risk-focused audit programs that respond to the possibility of red flags rather than assuming smooth execution. A risk-focused program does not simply list standard procedures by account area. It tailors those procedures to the conditions most likely to produce misstatement in the specific engagement. This requires linking known risks and likely warning signs to the audit procedures most capable of detecting them. For example, if the client has significant year-end sales pressure, the revenue program should include more detailed cutoff testing, contract review, post-period credit memo analysis, and confirmation procedures focused on unusual terms. If inventory is susceptible to valuation issues, the audit program should go beyond count observation and include testing of turnover, reserve methodologies, standard cost updates, and third-party custody arrangements. A well-designed program also allows the team to pivot when new red flags emerge. That flexibility is important, because risk assessments are not static. If a control appears weaker than expected or management explanations become inconsistent, the audit program should expand or shift accordingly. In practice, this means that audit programs should be structured with decision points in mind, so that staff know when a routine result becomes an exception requiring broader follow-up. A red-flag-oriented program is therefore dynamic rather than purely checklist-driven. It is designed not just to complete procedures, but to surface and investigate conditions that may signal heightened risk.

EXAMPLE

During the planning phase of an audit for a consumer electronics distributor, the auditor identified several engagement-specific risks: aggressive year-end sales targets, a history of inventory markdowns, and significant quantities of goods stored at third-party warehouses. Instead of relying on a standard audit program for revenue and inventory, the auditor designed procedures to address those specific red-flag risks. For revenue, the program included expanded cutoff testing for the final two weeks of the year, review of customer contracts for unusual acceptance or return terms, analysis of post-year-end credit memos, and confirmations targeted at large or unusual period-end transactions. For inventory, the program included the testing of turnover by product line, review of reserve calculations for obsolete goods, examination of recent standard cost changes, and confirmation of quantities held by outside logistics providers.

The program also built in decision points. For example, if post-year-end returns exceeded a defined threshold, the audit staff was instructed to expand sales testing and review additional customer correspondence. If count discrepancies or negative inventory balances were identified, they were to increase valuation testing and assess control weaknesses in inventory movement records.

As fieldwork progressed, those decision points became useful. Large returns on year-end shipments triggered more extensive testing, and the flexible program allowed the audit team to respond quickly to emerging red flags rather than remain limited to routine procedures.

Training the audit staff to identify warning signs is another essential part of this approach. Red flags are often first encountered by junior team members performing walkthroughs, vouching transactions, observing counts, or gathering support. If those individuals are trained only to complete tasks mechanically, important signals may be missed or dismissed as minor irregularities. Auditors need to understand what kinds of behavior, documentation issues, timing patterns, and account relationships should cause them to pause and ask questions. This training should include both technical and behavioral elements. They should know, for example, why a late round-dollar journal entry matters, why repeated delays in receiving documents may be significant, and why overly rehearsed management responses deserve attention. They should also understand that identifying a red flag is not the same as proving fraud. The purpose of raising the issue is to allow the team to evaluate it properly. A healthy audit culture encourages auditors to elevate unusual matters without fear of appearing inexperienced or disruptive. Training should therefore focus not only on what red flags look like, but also on how to communicate them clearly and promptly. The more effectively auditors are trained to recognize warning signs, the stronger the audit becomes at the point where evidence first enters the process.

Using data analytics to detect anomalies is also a powerful component of a red-flag-oriented audit approach. Modern audits often involve large populations of transactions, journal entries, user activity logs, and operational data that are too extensive to assess effectively through traditional manual review alone. Data analytics can help identify patterns that may indicate misstatement risk, such as unusual transactions posted near period-end, duplicate payments, gaps in sequencing, round-dollar entries, repeated overrides, changes in user access, or correlations that do not fit the business model. For example, analytics can isolate all journal entries posted on weekends by senior personnel, all receivables with rapidly increasing aging, or all inventory items with no movement but no reserve. They can also compare operational data to financial results in ways that highlight inconsistencies, such as revenue growth without corresponding shipment volume or payroll expense trends that do not align with headcount. The value of analytics is not merely speed. It is the ability to detect outliers and patterns that may not be visible through sample-based testing alone. However, analytics are useful only when interpreted thoughtfully. An anomaly is not automatically a red flag, and a red flag is not resolved simply because it is identified in a dashboard or report. The audit team must still evaluate the context, significance, and likely cause of the exception. Used properly, analytics strengthen the audit by making red flag detection more systematic and less dependent on chance observation.

EXAMPLE

During the audit of a multistate distributor, the auditor used data analytics to examine the full population of sales, receivables, journal entries, and inventory records rather than relying only on sample testing. The analysis identified several anomalies. A report of sales entries posted in the final three days of the year showed an unusual spike in round-dollar transactions entered by a small group of senior accounting personnel late at night. A separate analysis of receivables aging showed that many of those same customers already had overdue balances, yet no corresponding increase had been recorded in the allowance for doubtful accounts. Inventory analytics also highlighted a group of slow-moving items with no sales activity in nine months, but no obsolescence reserve had been assigned.

None of these items proved a misstatement by themselves, but together they created a pattern that warranted further work. The auditor followed up by examining the underlying contracts, reviewing post-year-end credit memos and cash receipts, and testing the journal entries supporting the year-end sales. Additional procedures showed that several transactions involved extended payment terms and contingent acceptance provisions, while some of the slow-moving inventory had been carried at full standard cost despite weak demand.

The analytics did not resolve the issue automatically, but they helped the auditor detect linked anomalies that might not have been visible through routine sampling alone.

Continuous improvement from prior audits is the final element in building a red-flag-oriented approach. Every audit generates information about where the client is vulnerable, how management responds to scrutiny, what controls tend to fail, and what types of issues recur. A strong audit team captures those lessons and uses them to improve future planning and execution. This does not mean assuming that prior-year conclusions remain valid automatically. Rather, it means using prior experience to sharpen awareness of recurring risks and to avoid relearning the same issues each year. For example, if the prior audit revealed repeated late adjustments in the close process, the current audit should plan earlier and more focused journal entry testing. If prior-year inventory counts produced large unexplained variances, the current team should prepare for more extensive count procedures and reserve analysis. If management previously resisted providing complete contract documentation, the team should anticipate that difficulty and respond more quickly when it reappears. Continuous improvement also involves internal reflection at the firm level. Audit teams should evaluate which red flags were identified late, which procedures were most effective, where skepticism could have been stronger, and how communication within the team worked in practice. These lessons can then be built into future methodology, templates, and staff training. A red-flag-oriented audit approach improves over time by learning from real engagements rather than treating each audit as though it begins from zero.

Taken together, these elements create a more disciplined and responsive audit process. Embedding red flags into planning helps the team know where problems are most likely to arise. Designing risk-focused programs ensures that procedures are aligned with those risks. Training the audit staff improves early detection. Data analytics expands the team's ability to see unusual patterns. Continuous improvement makes the process more effective from year to year. The common theme is that red flags should be part of the audit architecture, and not treated as incidental discoveries.

This kind of approach strengthens both effectiveness and efficiency. It improves effectiveness because the team is more likely to recognize meaningful warning signs before they become embedded in the audit file as unexplained exceptions. It improves efficiency because effort is directed toward the areas where unusual conditions are most likely to indicate material misstatement. Most importantly, it reinforces the idea that auditing is not just a process of verifying numbers. It is a process of evaluating whether the financial statements make sense in light of the underlying evidence, behavior, and circumstances of the entity. A red-flag-oriented audit approach keeps that purpose at the center of the engagement.

Summary

Auditing red flags are important because they rarely exist as isolated curiosities. They are signals that something in the financial reporting process, control structure, or underlying business activity may require closer attention. One of the key lessons from studying red flags is that unusual conditions do not prove misstatement by themselves, but they do require disciplined follow-up. A late journal entry, a weak reconciliation, a disputed receivable, an unexplained margin improvement, or an evasive management response may each have an innocent explanation. Even so, the auditor's responsibility is to investigate rather than assume. Another major lesson is that red flags are often most meaningful when viewed together. A single exception may be minor, but a pattern of documentation problems, aggressive estimates, control weaknesses, and management pressure can indicate a broader risk of material misstatement. Auditors also learn that professional skepticism is not limited to fraud situations. It applies equally to error, bias, incomplete disclosure, and management assumptions that may be technically plausible but economically weak. In many audits, the real challenge is not seeing the red flag. It is recognizing its significance before it is rationalized away.

A common auditor mistake in evaluating red flags is treating them too narrowly. Auditors sometimes view a warning sign as a one-time exception instead of asking whether it points to a larger issue. For example, one unsupported journal entry may be dismissed as poor documentation rather than recognized as a possible sign of management override. Another mistake is overreliance on management explanations. Management may provide a plausible reason for an unusual result, but if that explanation is not corroborated by reliable evidence, it should not end the inquiry. Auditors can also make the mistake of relying too heavily on prior-year conclusions, assuming that a client with no major issue in the past presents the same risk profile in the current year. Familiarity can reduce skepticism if the audit team stops reevaluating conditions with fresh judgment. Another recurring mistake is allowing deadlines or budget pressure to weaken follow-up. When unusual matters emerge late in the engagement, there can be a temptation to accept incomplete explanations in order to keep the audit moving. This is precisely when the quality of judgment matters most. Red flags lose their value when they are noticed but not pursued with sufficient seriousness.

In a strong audit culture, team members understand that raising concerns is part of professional responsibility, not a disruption of efficiency. Staff are encouraged to speak up when something seems inconsistent, even if they are not yet sure what it means. Managers and partners reinforce the idea that skepticism is not negativity. It is the disciplined habit of asking whether the evidence truly supports the conclusion. Vigilance also means staying alert throughout the audit, not just during planning or formal fraud discussions. Red flags can appear during walkthroughs, testing, inquiries, analytics, or final review, and the team needs to be prepared to respond at any stage. A culture of skepticism is also shaped by leadership. Senior auditors set the tone by how they react to questions, how seriously they treat unusual findings, and whether they reward careful thinking over mechanical completion. When skepticism and vigilance become part of the team's working habits, red flags are more likely to be recognized early, connected across audit areas, and resolved in a way that strengthens the reliability of the audit conclusion.

Glossary

A

Audit risk framework. The structure auditors use to identify where misstatements may occur and decide how much and what type of evidence is needed.

Auditing red flag. A condition, event, relationship, or behavior indicating that the auditor should examine an issue more closely because the risk of material misstatement may be elevated.

B

Bank reconciliation. A control procedure that compares a company's cash records with bank records to identify errors, timing differences, or unauthorized activity.

Bill-and-hold arrangement. A transaction in which the seller bills the customer before delivery while retaining possession of the goods.

C

Channel stuffing. The practice of pushing excess product to distributors or resellers near period-end to inflate current-period revenue.

Control environment. The foundation of internal control and reflects management's attitude toward integrity, accountability, and financial reporting discipline.

Control risk. The possibility that the entity's internal controls will fail to prevent or detect a misstatement on a timely basis.

E

Error risk. The risk of unintentional misstatement arising from mistakes such as mathematical errors, oversight, or incorrect application of accounting rules.

F

Fictitious sales. Recorded revenue transactions that never occurred or lack economic substance, often supported by false invoices or fabricated customer records.

Fraud risk. The risk of intentional deception that could lead to material misstatement, such as fictitious revenue, concealed liabilities, or altered records.

G

Going concern. The assumption that an entity will continue operating for the foreseeable future and will not be forced into liquidation or severe financial distress.

I

Inherent risk. The susceptibility of an assertion to misstatement before considering the effect of related internal controls.

K

Kiting. A scheme that exploits timing differences between bank accounts to overstate cash at period-end.

M

Management override. When those in authority bypass established controls through improper entries, altered estimates, or suppressed information.

P

Professional skepticism. A questioning mindset that requires the auditor to critically evaluate evidence rather than accept management explanations at face value.

R

Related-party transaction. A deal involving owners, executives, affiliates, family members, or controlled entities that may not occur on arm's-length terms.

Revenue recognition. The process of recording revenue when the applicable performance obligations have been satisfied and the recorded amount reflects the substance of the arrangement.

Risk of material misstatement. The chance that the financial statements are materially misstated before the auditor performs substantive procedures.

S

Segregation of duties. The separation of transaction initiation, recording, and custody responsibilities to reduce the opportunity for error or fraud.

T

Tone at the top. The ethical and control-oriented example set by senior leadership that influences behavior throughout the organization.

Index

Analytical procedure red flags.............. 63
Audit approach to spotting red flags... 102
Audit evidence red flags....................... 68
Audit risk framework 3

Case studies 98
Cash red flags 21
Communication of red flags 91
Control environment red flags.............. 10

Documentation of red flags 88

Entity-level risk assessment red flags... 13
Estimation red flags.............................. 45
Expense red flags.................................. 37

Fixed asset red flags 33
Fraud fundamentals 6

General ledger red flags........................ 41

Going concern red flags 54

Industry-specific red flags.....................76
Information technology red flags 59
Inquiry red flags 72
Inventory red flags 28

Liability red flags 37

Professional judgment...........................95

Receivables red flags 25
Related party red flags 49
Responses to red flags...........................84
Revenue recognition red flags...............17

Treasury red flags..................................21

Valuation red flags 45

www.ingramcontent.com/pod-product-compliance
Lightning Source LLC
LaVergne TN
LVHW082352200926
848481LV00012B/3546